LUCK, COINCIDENCE OR
PROVIDENCE?

A Foster Child's Journey through Racism,
Riots and Reggae to Faith

By Derek Morrison

Luck, Coincidence or Providence?

Author Derek Morrison

For information contact:
email: derekmorrison777@Yahoo.com

Cover design and Book layout by: AaronProductionsIndia.com

ISBN: 978-1-7398893-0-2

First Edition : December 2021

10 9 8 7 6 5 4 3 2 1

Contents

Foreword

There is one man who impressed me greatly when I walked into a London church. He knew his Bible and his demeanour was calm and humble. An inner peace and happiness oozed out of him. I discovered that his name is Derek Morrison and when he asked me to read his book it was a very easy choice. The book is intriguing because it allows the reader to travel with Derek through the bizarre events of his spiritual journey. A journey that has made Derek the person he is. There are plenty of intriguing, fun and engaging stories that you will thoroughly enjoy.

Dr Neale Schofield, former CEO of Adventist Media Network

Dedication

To my wife Joyce and my children Gregory and Gabriella.

Preface

It was July 2020; the churches were closed because of the global pandemic and I arranged a series of Zoom programmes at the church I attended. After discussing a programme with Marcia Mendoza, a health lecturer and practitioner, she asked how I came into the church. I shared a few stories that she enjoyed. Marcia then recommended I write my stories down for the future. Naturally, I did not take the suggestion seriously. However, a few months later, I felt impressed to do as she suggested, so I began the journey of creating this book of memoirs that I've titled *Luck, Coincidence, or Providence?: A Foster Child's Journey through Racism, Riots and Reggae to Faith.*

Acknowledgements

I would like to thank Imaan Wright, who helped transform my initial drafts that read like a business document into a book that narrates my thoughts and feelings. Credit also goes to Amanda Timmerman for her advice and editorial work, helping bring the manuscript to a published state. I'm grateful to Shaney and Derrick Bartley for beta reading and their valuable feedback helping me to dig even deeper. Finally, I'm also indebted to my son, Gregory Morrison, who played a part in proofreading and as a sounding board for the design of the front cover.

I've grouped the memoirs in this book into themes that roughly follows a chronological order of events and experiences. The dialogue between characters is true to intent.

BEING FOSTERED

Chapter 1

"There's no place like home."

Judy Garland
Actress

Who lives there?

"Why did you go in there?"

"I saw that white girl go in there," said a boy from Davidson High School.

"It's where I live, and she's my sister," I replied.

I felt it was unusual that they were so curious. To me, it was how it had always been.

My home on Davidson Road was between my school, South Norwood Juniors, and Davidson High School, which two older foster siblings attended. Leslie and Susan were six and five years older than me, respectively. We would walk home from school and approach home from opposite directions and the kids from Davidson High would see Sue walk into the house just before me. Naturally, this generated a host of questions like, "Do you live there?" "How come you've got a white sister?" Such questions became the norm.

Left Derek Morrison (1971/72)　　　　Right Susan Whitbread (Prudence)

A white working-class family fostered me in 1964, the same year I was born. We lived on Davidson Road in Croydon but moved to Ravensdale Gardens in Upper Norwood in 1975.

Ravensdale Gardens, was a small, newly built housing estate that was a cul-de-sac (dead end). Everyone moved into the estate at roughly the same time, so we had developed into a tight community where everyone knew everybody else and their business.

At Ravensdale Gardens, Sue dated Steve, who lived next door and was doing an apprenticeship as a printer. The two ended up eventually getting married. Steve was a walking encyclopaedia, you could talk to him about anything. Steve and Sue had friends who drove cars or rode motorbikes and they were always willing to drop me somewhere when I was going out. If I needed something ironed at the last minute, Sue was always willing to step up and help me out.

Leslie's girlfriend, Joan, coincidently moved into Ravensdale Gardens a few months after we did. Joan was a kind and generous woman who occasionally gave me a bit of money if she was around when I was getting ready to go out. Eventually Les and Joan got married.

Working with Big Brother

Les worked in a garage specialising in tyres and wheels and I often worked with him during the school holidays when I was around twelve. There was a mechanic there who had just left school. Let's call him Paul. He was roughly my height and build and made it a point to harass me verbally daily. When I complained to my brother, he said, "You have to stick up for yourself."

The mechanics would take it in turns to make tea for everyone; however, when it was Paul's turn to make tea, he did not make a cup for me. I asked him, "Where's mine?"

Paul looked me up and down and scoffed, "I'm not making one for you—make it yourself."

The other mechanics and Leslie continued as if nothing was wrong. I walked off into the yard and Paul came after me saying the usual things; that his former school, Tavistock, was harder (tougher) than my school, South Norwood High and that the boys from Tavy were better fighters. He then shoved me, hard, in the back, so I turned 180 degrees and, in one move, punched him in the face. His nose started to bleed. He tried to hit me back, but I moved out of the way, grabbed his hair and went to pull his head downwards onto my rising knee when my brother, who was six foot tall and well-built, stepped between Paul and me, grabbed Paul and dragged him away. The other mechanics saw what was happening and rushed over to hold me back. "Don't bleep touch him. I'm trying to get Paul out of Derek's way," Les said.

"Sorry Les, we thought you were going to hold Paul for Derek to hit him."

Paul went to wash the blood from his face. Later that day, he came over to me and said, "You're hard, mate," and shook my hand. Paul never bothered me again. On the way home Les said, "All those play fights we had taught you something then?"

My Foster Parents

My foster mother, Mary Prudence, was a domestic nurse and my foster father, Thomas Prudence, a lorry driver who spent some forty-odd years working for Cadbury Schweppes. Dad was the type of man who was never late for work.

They had met each other on a farm when the children were evacuated out of London during the Blitz of World War Two. They both had a love for animals, so growing up we had a range of different pets: the usual cats and dogs, birds, tortoises and at one point, a duck.

Derek and his foster mother (Mary Prudence), June 1981

My foster parents were quite liberal, open-minded to an extent, and generous people. They were not religious but had their own value system. My foster mother was a self-proclaimed atheist and my father claimed to be agnostic.

My dad was always fixing someone's bike or playing football with the boys in the neighbourhood. He loved watching TV (especially war films) and my mother loved reading books (romantic period drama and crime novels).

Our front door was pretty much always open. Certain children from down the street were allowed to just walk into our kitchen and eat more or less much what they fancied.

From left to right: Derek, behind him Leslie, Susan, and Dad (Thomas Prudence) holding Robert. Petticoat Lane market around 1969

I remember kids who ran away from home would come to my house and my mother would give them a little pocket money and some sweets, listen to what they had to say, then encourage them to return home.

If my friends came around for me and I was not in, they sometimes hung around and had tea and biscuits with my mother or a can of Pepsi Cola and some chocolates before they went on their way. Because my dad worked for Cadbury Schweppes, there were always sweets and soft drinks around the house, which he got from work on staff discount.

I remember on more than one occasion coming home from school and saying something like, "Mum, I got detention next week Monday."

"Why?"

"Talking in class."

"You'll learn the hard way."

Another time, I said, "Mum, got detention next week Monday."

"Why?"

"Richard and I were running in the corridor."

"What's wrong with you? I suppose if Richard jumped in front of a double-decker bus you'd do the same thing. If I've told you once, I've told you a thousand times not to copy what other people are doing!"

I quickly learnt to either not report my misbehaviour or, if it was of a magnitude where the school was going to write a letter to my parents, I made sure to report my version of events first, without mentioning anybody else.

I recall coming home and describing the clothes I saw people wearing.

"Mum, George has got crocodile skin shoes and belt."

"You don't know what he did to get the money to buy that stuff. He may have hit an old lady over the head and stole her pension money or sold himself as a male prostitute for the night to make some fast cash, is that what you want to do?"

"No!"

"Well, if you want something, go out and work for it!"

Younger Siblings in the Family

After my arrival, there were three more additions to the family: My foster parents adopted an Anglo-Indian baby called Robert. He's three years younger than me. He too joined the family as a baby. Robert hung around with the kids from down the road who were my age and played for the Ravensdale Gardens football team that my dad and other fathers from the street organised and ran.

Lisa, who was born into the family in 1968, followed Robert. As a child, Lisa would deliberately stand in front of the TV when our favourite programmes were on. We'd call out, "Mum, Lisa is standing in front of the TV again."

The standard reply was, "She'll soon get bored and move out of the way if you take no notice of her." I'd protest to my foster mother and she'd say, "The more you fuss the more she'll do it, ignore her and she'll stop."

"Yeah but, Mum, can't you just tell her to get out of the way?"

Then my mum would ignore me.

The final addition to the family was Jason, who was born a year after Lisa. As a kid Jason was into his CB radio, riding his BMX bike and roller skating with his friends from off the street.

From left to right: Derek, Lisa, Jason and Robert, around 1979

Childhood Photographs

Dad, Mum, Leslie, Susan and Derek
about 1965/66

Dad and Derek on holiday about 1965/66

From left to right Derek, Les, Dad, Robert in the pram, Sue
about 1968 at Selsey holiday camp

From left to right: Les (holding Lisa), Derek,
Mum (holding Jason), Sue (1969/70)

Derek with Leslie and Susan birthday celebrations about 1967/68

Derek and Sue in her Girls Brigade uniform back
garden at Davidson road

My Natural Parents

My biological mother, Monica Morrison, 1968

My biological mother (Monica Morrison, also known as Daphne Morrison) was from a rural part of St Catherine, Jamaica whereas my biological father, who I never met and whose name I don't know, was Nigerian according to my foster mother. Monica was studying to take her nursing exams during my younger years but visited as often as possible. She lived in Stoke Newington, fifteen miles away on the other side of London.

When I was about five or six, Monica moved to Canada and eventually settled in New York to further her nursing career, no doubt on a quest to set up a home and a family. I have a younger blood sister called Joanna, who is identical in age to Lisa.

Growing up, not knowing any of my blood relatives did not bother me as my life was content and enjoyable. My passion was playing basketball and being one of the top players in the school team gave me a sense of achievement. Representing the school at swimming galas made me feel like I was following in the footsteps of my older siblings. Going on bike rides with my friends and getting into the usual childish mischief created a combination of excitement and fear. Playing chess with my dad and eventually being able to beat him and my school teachers was rewarding. However, knowing my dad, he probably deliberately allowed me to win, occasionally, to encourage me.

Meanwhile, Monica dated and eventually married a Jamaican man, Mr Campbell (I don't know his first name), who lived in East London. While she was in Canada and New York, Mr Campbell would come to visit me and I'd have to go up to where he lived in Clapton, East London to see him. Looking back, I can say he was a decent man. But I felt he was odd and very different from my foster parents, who I regarded as marvellous.

Visits

Before Monica went to Canada and New York, when she was in England, she would come and visit me and phone beforehand. My foster mother would inform me by saying, "Your mother's coming on such and such a day and time," which was code for make sure you comb your hair properly or I'll do it for you. That would have been an unpleasant experience for me. My foster brother Leslie's hair was straight and a comb just glided through it, while my hair was thick and curly and the only way to get it looking neat was to painfully force a comb through the tight curls.

When Monica visited, she would always tell me to read the Bible and go to church. This happened from since I can remember until I was around nine years old. However, attending church was not something I was overly keen on doing.

My older sister, Sue, used to go to church as part of her Girls' Brigade club. Occasionally, I went along with her because, as a kid, anywhere she and Les went I wanted to go too. That said, I didn't have a clue what was going on in the church. At age nine or ten, I joined the Boys' Brigade with my friends, Derek Chambers and Ben Shaw. We'd have to go to church for parades, but again, what was said and done all went over the top of my head.

There were three Christian storybooks in my house. I got the impression they were mine, but I wasn't allowed to have them for some unknown reason. They were put away in my parents' bedroom cupboard.

Being a typical youngster (around eight or nine at the time), the very thing I was told I couldn't have I wanted. So when my parents weren't looking or were out, I would go and get the books and look at the pictures. I loved looking at the pictures. One of the books had a picture of a statue of a metallic man with his arms folded. Each segment of his body (head, arms, thighs, legs and feet) was a different colour.

One day, Sue caught me with the books open and said teasingly that the books were hers.

I said, "No they're not!"

The initials SP were on the back of the books, which she said proved that the books were hers and not mine. SP, she claimed, stood for Susan Prudence (her initials). It irritated me no end, but what could I do? Neither of us should have had them in the first place.

I'm Not Sure What to Call You

Monica returned to England when I was eleven (1975). I felt uneasy whenever she visited because I was unsure what to call her since I addressed my foster parents as Mum and Dad. However, to call my biological mother anything else other than Mum seemed wrong. Nevertheless, it felt unnatural to call her Mum, so I didn't. To solve this problem, I implemented a strategy that limited what I said to my biological mother in the presence of my foster family—that way, I would not have to say "Mum" to attract Monica's attention. Conversely, when Monica and I were alone, I made sure I got eye contact or attracted her attention some other way before saying anything to avoid having to say, "Mum."

One day I decided to try to call Monica "Mum." I was at her home in East London; I waited for the opportunity; I felt the roof of my mouth and my throat dry up, my lips felt slightly tight. I looked towards Monica and forced the word "Mum" out of my mouth. It must have sounded as soft as a butterfly flapping its wings. Monica did not respond, so I guessed she did not hear. It felt so artificial, so I did not try it again.

Where Do You Come From?

I remember being in South Norwood Junior School at age nine (1973) I was in conversation with Samuel Bascomb and he said that his parents were from Barbados and that he was from Barbados. So I asked him, "Am I from Barbados?"

"Yes, of course."

I went home and announced, "Mum, I'm from

Barbados."

"Where did you get that from?"

"Sam said we are all from Barbados."

"Your mother isn't from Barbados, she's from Jamaica,

and you were born in and come from England."

How Did You Get Here?

The same year (1973), I heard some girls singing in the playground:

"My Bonnie lies over the ocean

My Bonnie lies over the sea

My mummy laid over my daddy

And that's how they got little me."

I thought, *That's not what happened to get me.*

When I got home, I said to my foster mum, "Mum, why am I fostered?"

"Well, your mum comes from a small village in the Jamaican countryside, she was very bright at school, top of her class, so the people in the village saved up their money and gave it to her so she could come to England to study to be a nurse. She got pregnant with you and decided to put you into a foster home with a family so you would have brothers and sisters to play with. She wouldn't have been able to study and pass her nursing exams and look after a baby. The villagers did not have a lot of money, and it would have all been lost if she didn't finish her studies."

"Um... Can I go out to the park?"

My Name

One day, my foster mother said she wanted to talk to me. I thought, *This sounds serious.* The usual protocol was that she'd just say what was on her mind without laying the groundwork. We sat down alone in the living room and she said, "You know Mr Campbell and your mum are getting married."

"Yeah?"

"Well, they would like you to change your name to Campbell."

"I don't want to."

"Do you want to think about it?"

"No... I don't want to change my name."

The topic was not spoken about again.

I felt that changing my name would have been like betraying myself.

Concerns of an Eleven-Year-Old

At eleven years old, life was pretty much carefree. My biggest concerns were: could I beat my dad the next time we played chess? Would we win our next basketball match? Would the weekly shopping include the odd-tasting supermarket low-budget cornflakes or the more popular brand? And could I get my homework completed correctly and handed in on time? However, events were about to change that would dwarf my so-called "biggest concerns" and really give me something to worry about.

A Revealing Doctor's Appointment

One Saturday in the autumn of 1975, when I was eleven years old, I spent the day with Mr Campbell in East London. He took me to get a haircut and then to get my photograph taken. Monica would be visiting the UK and I assumed the haircut was to ensure I looked neat and tidy when she arrived.

A few months later, I was with my foster parents and younger siblings driving around doing the usual family errands, one of which included a trip to the doctor's to pick up a prescription. The nurse said to my foster mother, "I hope Derek enjoys his holiday."

"Holiday! What holiday?"

"He's going abroad to Jamaica, isn't he?"

"Jamaica—says who?"

"Mr Campbell was in here last week to get a signature for Derek's passport photograph."

"Well, that's the first I've heard of it."

My mother left the doctor's surgery and got in the car.

"What's this about you getting a passport and going off to Jamaica?"

"Passport? I know nothing about a passport," I replied

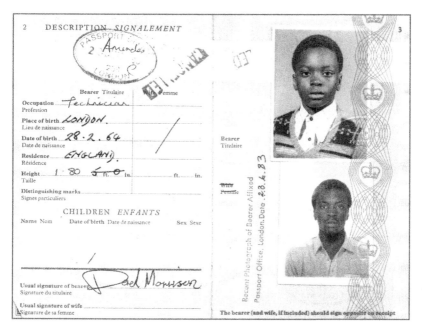

My original passport dated September 1975 at age eleven - updated in 1983

My mum and dad discussed the issue; however, it was clear to us all what was going on. It would have been a one-way ticket to New York via Jamaica.

"How did Mr Campbell get a photograph of you for a passport?" my mother said.

"A few weeks ago," I said, "when Mr Campbell took me for a haircut—"

"And you did not think to say anything?" she said.

31

I thought to myself, *This is a trick question; there's no right answer.* So I kept my mouth shut.

My mum mused for a while then said, "Do you want to go?"

"No!"

"What did you ask him that for?" my dad said.

My mum replied, "It's no good me kicking up a fuss about keeping him here if he turns around at the last minute and says he wants to go."

My foster mother and biological mother, Monica, had several frank discussions. It concluded with Monica giving my passport to my foster mother and promising not to take me away from my foster family, home and school. She also reassured me that I would never be taken away from my home.

Unsettling Times

Sometime later, in early 1976, there was an unexpected knock on the door. They served my foster parents with court papers. Monica had set in motion court proceedings so she could have custody over me.

The few months between being served with papers and the court case were tense. I was a mischievous kid and my foster parents forbade me to get into any trouble because the school would need to produce a report about me that would be reviewed in the court case.

Monica came and visited from the time the papers were served right until the court case. We hardly exchanged words. I did not want to leave my school, friends, basketball team, brothers or sisters, or foster mum and dad. I resented the situation and felt it was all quite unfair.

My dad, who was a quiet and reserved person, constantly reassured me by saying things like, "This is your home," and, "It'll always be your home, the door is always open—only just don't get on an aeroplane."

Eventually, the week of the court case came. My foster parents' lawyer said the case would take four days. From the outset, they had cautioned that the chances of me staying in my foster home were slim because I was not adopted, so my foster parents had no legal right to keep me, even though I had been with them since I was nine months old.

Day One of the Court Case

There were several discussions between my mum, dad and older brother and sister after the first day of court proceedings. Then my mother turned to me and said, "I don't care what they say, get your suit ready, you're coming to court for day three— and you can tell them what you think and want."

I was told at the outset that I would not go to court and would not need to take the stand. I figured out that things must be going badly if I had to pitch in. I felt quite frightened about the whole affair. It was hard enough having to walk on eggshells while I was at school. I'd already had someone come around to visit me, asking me all types of questions, no doubt psychoanalysing my every answer, facial expression and body movement. Now I had to go to court and be questioned yet again—I did not relish the prospect at all. I felt nervous about the whole affair; I worried that one wrong answer might ruin things.

Day Two of the Court Case

That night, after day two, my parents came home with the news that the judge had made his decision. I was made a Ward of Court; I could not leave the country or get married before I was eighteen without the court's permission, and, most of all, I was to remain in my home with my foster parents and siblings.

The closer it got to the court case the more I worried. What would I do if the judge did not rule in my favour? Would I run away? If so, where would I go? What would I eat? How would I live? I felt deeply relieved that it was all over, back to normal, and my parents were delighted.

Two or three years after the case, I remember being in my parents' bedroom and looking out the window, pondering what my life would have been like if the court case had gone sour. My dad walked in and asked what I was doing. I turned with tears in my eyes and thanked him.

Sometime after the court case, Monica and Mr Campbell just vanished—they were nowhere to be found. The whole incident caused a lot of bitterness between my foster parents and biological mother. However, my foster mother would periodically say, "Monica is your mother; she clearly loves you, she's just gone about showing it in a peculiar way. The argument is between me and her. She's your mother and she loves you; you are not to get involved."

To which I would answer, "Yes, Mum."

My Name Revisited

Around six months after the court case, my foster mother said she wanted to talk about something. "Your dad and I would like to adopt you."

"What does that mean?"

"Your name would change to Prudence."

"I don't want to change my name."

My foster mother took a long draw on her cigarette, exhaled, slightly nodded and said, "All right then," barely moving her lips.

Life continued as if the conversation had never happened.

So that's a summary of my life up until age thirteen. The rest of this memoir will cover, some aspects, of my teenage years from thirteen through to nineteen.

MY WORLD OF ROOTS ROCK REGGAE

Chapter 2

Wanting to Be a Rastaman

The year was 1977 and inflation was approximately 15.8%. High inflation over the past three years had pushed prices up by nearly 70%. The National Front (an extreme right-wing, racist political party) clashed with anti-Nazi protesters when they marched in London. *Roots*, a TV miniseries, was aired on British television.

Roots was based on Alex Haley's book by the same name and tells the story of how Haley traces his lineage (seven generations) from his present day right back to the first slave in his family,

Kunta Kinta, who was taken captive from West Africa and arrived in America in 1767.

Meanwhile, I'd entered my teenage years and remembered saying to my foster mother, "Mum, I want to be a Rastaman. I want to grow dreadlocks."

"Oh no you're not!"

"Why?"

"What do you think is going to happen when you walk down the street and the old bill see you?" "Old bill" is a slang term for the police.

"Yeah, but—"

"Don't *but* me. I said no! How do you suppose you'll get a job with your hair like some Rastaman?"

Wanting to grow dreadlocks was a topic of contention and caused periodic disagreements at home, mainly because in the '70s, in many quarters, dreadlocks were socially unacceptable, even in the Afro-Caribbean community. For example, certain nightclubs would not allow you admittance. In addition, the older Caribbean community frowned on Rastamen, and my parents felt dreadlocks were an added target for the police.

Miss Brown, who taught religious education, gave the class an assignment where we had to research a religion with a partner and write an essay. I teamed up with my best friend, Richard Harry, and we decided to explore Rastafarianism. I ended up doing the research and write-up on my own. Richard's father ran his own business, had company premises down the road from our school, drove a Jaguar, and was always dressed in a suit and a tie. He objected to Richard researching Rastafarianism.

Reasons for Wanting to Be a Rastaman

A few of the experiences I had as a child and teenager corresponded with the messages about Rastafarianism I heard in the reggae music I had listened to.

Back in 1972/1973, at around eight or nine years old, I was walking home after school and took a shortcut through a car park. As I exited and was walking down the road, a police car pulled up. The policeman stopped me and, in a bullish manner, asked what I was doing and why I was walking through the car park. He suggested I was breaking into cars, which was the furthest thing from my mind. Eventually, he let me go, but I was still feeling quite frightened when I got home. This was my first encounter with the police and I was too scared to tell my parents what had happened because I should not have been taking that route home. So I kept the incident to myself.

On another occasion, around 1975/1976, Richard Harry and I were walking through Croydon High Street in broad daylight when plainclothes police officers pushed us up against the wall. They told us to empty our pockets and questioned us and then told us to go home or else. I openly admit that, as teenagers, there were times when we were up to mischief and police intervention would have been appropriate. The general reception black teenagers received from society (which Rastafarians labelled as Babylon) was one of suspicion. My contemporaries and I regularly experienced being followed around departmental stores by undercover shop assistants. If you sat near a lady on public transport, she would pick up her handbag and hold it in such a way as if she was expecting you to snatch it from her.

The experiences with the police and society in general corresponded to messages in reggae music that the police were the wicked-man part of the Babylonish system of oppression. Growing up, the only time I felt safe when police officers were around was when the local football team, Crystal Palace, was playing at home. The police who filled the street were preoccupied with crowd control rather than monitoring every move black teenagers made.

Some aspects of reggae songs were:

"Babylon ah put on the pressure oh yes, hard time

pressure, on this land"

by Sugar Minott;

"Police and thieves in the street, ooh yes, scaring the

nation with their guns and ammunition"

by Junior Murvin;

"War in inna Babylon, tribal war inna Babylon"

by Max Romeo

"Babylon don't like this man, even though his done no wrong... because his a Rastaman a true born African, because his a Rastaman and his awaiting repatriation, repatriation."

by Carl Malcom.

Listening to such lyrics gave me a sense of reassurance in the teachings of Rastafarianism.

In 1975/1976, I was eleven and in the first year of secondary school (South Norwood High). I remember being in a science class and learning from Ms White for the first time that pork carried parasites, in particular the tapeworm. We sketched a picture of the tapeworm in our exercise-books and described how it grew and consumed all the food a person ate until they died.

The thought of eating but constantly feeling hungry and eventually dying of starvation made me feel quite uneasy. So from that point onwards, I stopped eating pork.

I announced this to my foster parents, who did not take too kindly to it. Probably because during and after the Second World War, they experienced rationing due to the shortage of food available. Like all good mothers, my mother would search for bargains so that her family had as many luxuries as possible, including roast pork for Sunday dinner.

Around 1976 I also learnt through discussions with friends that Rastamen did not eat pork. That resonated with me deeply. I also liked that if I grew dreadlocks, I would not have to go through the discomfort of combing my hair. Both were good reasons to embrace Rasta ideology.

As 1977 entered, I became even more interested in Rastafarianism. Coupled with the opinions I had built up about the police came the ideology of repatriation back to Africa. This concept grabbed my attention because the National Front spread the propaganda that black people did not belong here in Great Britain. That was emphasised with so-called jokes that were told like, "Just because a dog is born in a stable it does not make him a cow, so just because a black person is born in Britain does not make him British," which added to the National Front's narrative that black people didn't belong here.

In the '70s, some TV programmes also perpetuated an unpleasant feeling towards black people in the UK. One such was *Love Thy Neighbour*. It featured a white couple who lived next door to a black couple. The white man played the part of an ignorant racist who constantly suggested that the black man next door should "go home".

A common question I was asked (in fact, one I have been asked throughout my teenage and adult life) was, "Where are you from?" Of course, my standard reply was always, "Croydon."

Years later, a comedian called Jim Davidson had a make-believe black friend he called 'Chalky', the butt of all his jokes. While my mind was already made up, comedians like Jim Davidson just reinforced the feeling that black people didn't belong in Britain and validated the idea that Rastafarianism must be right.

I remember seeing on TV that Idi Amin had expelled all Indians from Uganda, and, being a child, I thought expelling all ethnic minorities was the order of the day. I remember asking my mum, "If all the black people are told to leave England, can I stay?"

I was born and raised in England and loved it. I loved attending South Norwood High, and I loved my family, but there were several external signals, good and bad, outside of home and school that kept on saying, "You don't belong here."

I picked up sound bites in reggae songs such as

"Africa, our fathers' land is calling us home"

sung by the group The Mighty Diamonds.

"Looking out the window daydreaming of Africa building up a great civilisation"

by Lloyd Jones and

"Took us away from civilisation, brought us to slave in this big plantation…"

by the Abyssinians.

All added to the narrative that black people did not belong in Britain.

I loved listening to reggae music; one of my favourite songs was called "True Rastaman" by the artist Fred Locks. The song speaks about what Jah (another name for God) says a dedicated Rastaman should be like.

The words to the first verse are:

So Jah say

Rasta don't work for no CIA

Jah sent us here to show the way, oh yeah

Rasta don't work for no politician

True Rastaman is a good and upright man

So he will live, yes he'll live forevermore

Through Jah mercy, he'll endure

The whole idea of being a good and upright person was appealing to me. We were taught that at school, and my (foster) grandmother strongly promoted that way of living.

All things considered, I felt that what Rastas taught spoke to my experience and aligned to my thinking and I was persuaded both emotionally and intellectually to adopt the Rastafarian ideology.

Sound Systems the Vehicle of Reggae Music

One day, around summer 2020, I was talking with my daughter, Gabriella, a mature student, and she told me that someone in her PhD group was doing a doctorate in reggae music.

From thirteen to sixteen, I was very much into sound systems, reggae music and nightlife. So, wanting to demonstrate to my daughter that I was once an expert in reggae music, I segued the conversation by asking her if she knew what a sound system was. She replied yes, so I asked her to explain it to me. Technically her explanation was correct, but it was not the answer I was looking for. So, I explained the concept of a reggae sound system based on my 1970s experience.

You could consider a sound system as consisting of two parts: the personnel and the equipment. The personnel would comprise of MCs (masters of ceremonies), DJs (disc jockeys, commonly termed "the selectors"), and those who carried the boxes into the venue and cabled up the system. MCs would introduce the music being played and would voice over the song. This was typically a combination of singing and reciting his unique poetical lyrics, consisting of rhyming couplets and triplets that harmonised with the music being played. DJs would decide what music was played—in essence, they defined the playlist for the evening.

Hardware would comprise of custom, primarily homemade, equipment such as amplifiers, special effects audio equipment, and speaker boxes. Speaker boxes ranged from four to six feet tall and would contain anything from one to four eighteen-inch speakers. The bigger boxes would be fitted with bass speakers. Smaller speaker boxes were placed on top of the bass boxes, these smaller boxes would give you the tenor sound (commonly called mid-range), and then sitting on top of those were even smaller boxes that gave you the high-frequency treble sound.

The concept of sound systems originated in Jamaica and was introduced to the UK by those who migrated here from that island. By the 1970s/80s, there were probably a hundred plus sound systems across England, each with their name, unique way of playing music and cult following.

The popularity of an individual sound system would be down to several factors: the DJ's ability to select an appropriate record, often in response to a song that another sound system had just finished playing; the quality of the equipment that produced the audible sound; the way the song was introduced and mixed between bass, mid-range, and treble at the appropriate juncture and the talent of the MC in voicing over the music with his lyrics.

You could group sound systems into different categories based on the genres of reggae music they predominantly played. For example, some sounds played mostly lovers' rock (romantic music) or soft, carefree reggae music. Others played light-hearted cultural music about everyday life and still others would focus on and be known for playing hard-core, roots-rock-reggae that had a political or revolutionary bias.

Roots-rock-reggae also promoted the Rastafarianism ideology. The songs frequently used phrases, verses and terminology from the Bible. Often a blend of different genres would be played depending on the venue, occasion and time of night.

Places I Went to Listen to Reggae Music

By the age of twelve, I'd left the Boys' Brigade and started going to discos at the local YMCA, where the music played was either soul or disco. Towards the end of the evening, they would play one or two popular reggae songs, which I looked forward to hearing all night long.

One Friday night in 1976, I was at a YMCA disco and went to the toilets only to see a small crowd of teenagers. I wondered,

What is everyone looking at? Then, out of curiosity, I walked towards the group to see for myself.

There was Felix with a pack of cigarette papers. He had joined a few of the papers together. My dad used cigarette papers to smoke his tobacco because it was cheaper than buying cigarettes, but I'd never seen him join multiple papers together. I was puzzled as to why Felix would do that, so I continued to watch.

He then took out a pack of cigarettes, took one out and broke roughly a third of it off and sprinkled the tobacco into the cigarette paper. I thought, *That's stupid. Why not just smoke the cigarette as it is?* Then I saw him pull out a small bag with dark green stuff in it and sprinkle some of it on top of the tobacco. It then dawned on me what it was.

Weed. I'd never seen weed or any type of drugs before. My heart started to beat faster and harder. I left the toilets right away.

By age thirteen (1977), I'd graduated to dance halls (where sound systems played) beginning with a place we called Parchmore in Thornton Heath and later a nightclub called Rainbow in East Croydon.

At Parchmore, where the people were much older, I became accustomed to the smell of weed, which I quite liked. It had a pleasant fragrance, unlike the harsh smell of cigarettes, which I disliked. Periodically, someone would ask me to hold out my hand so they could assemble their spliff in my palm. I would watch with interest and study every action as they joined the papers together, sprinkled the tobacco and weed in the paper adding more substance to one end, then removed it from my hand and rolled it in such a way as to create a cone-shaped spliff. Then they would give me a slight nod to say thank you. Being asked made me feel like an adult.

Following and Joining a Sound System

I became fascinated with sound systems. Richard Harry and I would travel across London to listen to a sound we had not heard before. If Richard could not make it, then I'd go on my own and look forward to telling him, with glee, all about it at school Monday morning, describing the speaker boxes, the music, and the excitement of the dance.

Eventually, I started going to dance halls with my older friends, mainly Anthony Campbell and Derek Chambers. Anthony knew a lot about reggae music and sound systems because his aunt dated a man who owned Lord David, a top sound system from Battersea. So Anthony as a young teenager would tag along with his aunt when she went out to various clubs.

Derek Chambers was close friends with Michael Rennie, brother of Cecil, who owned King Tubby's, a top sound system from Brixton. Derek introduced me to King Tubby's, and on occasions I'd go along with him and his friends to listen to them. Michael had moved into Croydon from Brixton. We'd go around his house during the week, hang out in his bedroom and listen to music. Then, around ten o'clock, he'd ask us to go; if we were slow in responding, he'd lock his bedroom door and take out a selection of old-fashioned, early seventies reggae records (which we did not like) and play them for an hour or so till we begged him to let us go.

Anthony and Michael would debate enthusiastically, reminiscing about which sound was the first to play a particular dub plate (exclusive reggae music that sound systems would order directly from recording studios in Jamaica), the venue it was played and how the crowd reacted. But, of course, each had their specific bias on which sound was the best.

I soaked it all in like a sponge; consequently, my knowledge and passion for the sound systems business and Reggae music continued to deepen.

In 1977, a newly launched Rasta sound system from Battersea called Moa Anbessa (Amharic for "Conquering Lion") played in a blues party on Clifton Road, South Norwood. I remember Anthony telling us about Moa Anbessa, how they had split away from Lord David and were now one of the hottest sound systems in London. At blues parties, you paid a 50p entrance fee and you'd have to buy the food and drink. There was commonly at least one person at the party selling weed. The Observer, or some other local sound system, was playing music until Moa Anbessa turned up.

I remember watching the Rastamen in Moa Anbessa enter the house, bringing in speaker boxes through the windows because the party was already packed out. The boxes were as tall as wardrobes, cabling the speakers to the valve amplifiers and then playing reggae music. The bass was deep, mellow, and undistorted, which caused the entire house to vibrate in sync with the rhythm of the music being played. That, accompanied by a treble that was both sharp, crisp, and crystal-clear, reverberated through the building along with the bass to add an extra touch of class and quality that I had not heard in a sound system before. The ultimate touch to this experience was how Moa Anbessa used an echo chamber to reinforce the messages of the MC in a unique way. Being of an impressionable age, I instantly fell in love with it all.

While my friends and I listened to many sound systems across London, we gravitated towards Moa Anbessa. In 1978, we eventually became part of the team. We did this by turning up to the dance halls early and offering to lift the speaker boxes out of the truck and into the hall for them as a means of getting into the venue without paying.

Within three months, we were fully integrated into the sound system, travelling far and wide, spending all night listening to music.

One Saturday night, in 1978, we had just finished carrying boxes into a blues party. Music started to play. However, it was still early, so people had not turned up. A Rastaman I knew well gave me some weed, so I assembled a spliff and smoked it. The feeling it gave me only added to the enjoyment of listening to the music, so from then on, every time I went out, I continued to indulge in smoking weed.

Being part of a sound system taught me a few things about business.

Berris, who was probably in his mid-twenties and was the DJ and joint owner of the sound, periodically took me behind the scenes and exposed me to the financial side of things. As a result, I came to appreciate that records needed to be purchased, equipment bought and maintained, deposits on venues had to be paid, and the truck also required maintenance it did not run itself.

Meanwhile, Clive and Jagger who were also joint owners of Moa Anbessa taught me the rewards of promoting and marketing a dance. We'd drive during the day, in Jagger's Ford Capri, to shopping centres, hairdressers and barbers to distribute leaflets that advertised dances. Then we'd give leaflets out at clubs and dance halls. I quickly learnt that the effort put into promote a dance was directly proportional to the number of people that turned up at the event, providing you got the other basics right.

The top three London sound systems owned and run by Rastas during my day (1977 to 1980) were Sir Coxsone, Jah Shaka, and Moa Anbessa. Often these three sounds played together; as I listened to their selection of music, my stance in the Rastafarianism belief system increased.

Berris
Moa Anbessa's DJ 1979.

Derek Chambers, Errol Spence
and Colin Ming 1979

The Sunday Observer Magazine

Sunday 9 April 1978 I was hanging out on Carmichael Road, Anthony Campbell, who had joined Moa Anbessa the same time as me, said, "Hey, you want to be a Rastaman—you should read this," as he thrust the *Observer* Sunday supplement magazine in my hands.

I looked at the front cover and began to flick through the pages. I thought. *This is amazing.*

Anthony then said, "You can't keep it."

The featured article was entitled "The Rastafarians: A vision of repatriation" with a few photographs of Rastamen in Jamaica.

1979 Some of the group of us that joined Moa Anbessa sound system in 1978
From left to right: Derek Morrison, Errol Spence, Everton Bennett,
Derek Chambers, Dice and Andrew Morris.

October 2021 at Derek Chamber's Funeral. Part of the group that joined
Moa Anbessa in 1978. From left to Right Derek Morrison, Errol Spence,
Everton Bennett, Colin Ming and Andrew Morris

I was not an avid reader, but I read this article. I saw another side of Rastafarianism: Rastas who decided to live a natural life, up in the hills, away from commercialisation and the violence of city life—it was akin to a hippie commune minus the free love aspect. The imagery of Rastas smoking a chalice (peace pipe) gave me a thirst for wanting to do the same thing. I'd never seen a chalice in real life, let alone smoked one.

I wrote to the *Observer* newspaper to see if they had any additional information on Rastafarianism that they could send me. But unfortunately they were only able to send a copy of the original magazine. I treasured that I had my own copy and periodically reread facts about Rastafarianism. The crucial Rasta doctrine was that the late Ethiopian emperor, Haile Selassie (1930 to 1974), was God/Jah, the Messiah for black people; this ideology came about because the late Marcus Garvey (1887 to 1940), who was a Jamaican political activist and entrepreneur amongst other things, prophesied that black people should look to Africa where a black king shall be crowned, he shall be the redeemer. Following Garvey's statements, Haile Selassie ascended the throne.

As I read the magazine, I would daydream of going to Jamaica and immersing myself in the abundance of low-cost if not free weed, listening to top sound systems with high profile reggae artists voicing over the music and sitting down and learning from the Rastamen.

Hanging Out with Rastamen

My friends, who joined Moa Anbessa at the same time as me, were older and had full-time jobs while I was still at school. So during the school holidays, I would go up to Wandsworth and Battersea one or two days per week and hang out with some of the Rastas in Moa Anbessa. They introduced me to their friends, which naturally increased the number of Rastamen I was acquainted with.

One of the dichotomies I found as I sought to learn more about Rastafarianism was that some Rastamen would encourage me to read and be educated culturally. Yet, they also taught that the Bible could not be understood because it had been changed by the white man (or so they said). Rastafarianism taught that the late Emperor Haile Selassie was God and that his proper biblical name was "Jah", as found in the King James Version of the Bible. Psalm 68:4 says:

> *"Sing unto God, sing praises to his name: extol him that rideth upon the heavens by his name Jah, and rejoice before him."*

However, the same Psalm in another version of the Bible would not have the name Jah but "Lord", as in the Revised Standard Version (RSV) of the Bible:

"Sing to God, sing praises to his name; lift up a song to him who rides upon the clouds; his name is the Lord, exult before him!"

This difference in name was presented to me as proof that the Bible had been changed.

Another example used to show the truth was being hidden was the belief that some of the books of the Bible had been taken out. For example, the books of the Apocrypha were not included as part of the Bible. Rastafari taught that these books and more had been left out to hide the true identity of the black man: God's specially chosen people.

So, when I heard Rasta sound systems like Moa Anbessa play songs such as "What about the Half" by the late reggae singer Dennis Brown, it seemed to all fit together. The words to the first verse of the song are:

We got to know the truth

What about the half that's never been told?

What about the half that's never been told?

Look how long it's been kept a big secret

Look how long it's been hidden away

The half, the half, the half that's never been told

The half, the half, the half that's never been told

What is hidden from the wise and good

It shall reveal to babe and suckling

The half, the half, the half that's never been told.

The song was played with a rhythmic beat, with the base being as deep as thunder that vibrated through your body like a shockwave; it seemed to influence and indoctrinate the listeners.

Was Haile Selassie the True and Living God?

To me, the music, sound systems, Selassie, Rastafarianism, all linked together like a chain. However, I'd periodically hear about a Rastaman who cut his dreadlocks because he no longer believed Selassie was God. I remember being with Derek Chambers and Everton Bennett, who were both in the Moa Anbessa sound; they challenged me on the topic and I could not defend my point of view. Purposefully, I began a quest to deepen my knowledge. I did not like the feeling of not being able to fully explain what I believed.

There was an Ethiopian boy named Caleb who was in my year at school. I asked him what he knew about Emperor Haile Selassie. To my surprise, he said that his father used to work for Selassie as a diplomat. As a consequence, we got into several discussions. He was genuine and brought a photograph album to school with pictures of Selassie and his father.

The photographs were amazing. I'd never seen those particular prints before! Pictures of Haile Selassie were quite common in record shops, on album covers, in framed pictures in dance halls, on posters on the walls in friends' bedrooms etc., hence the somewhat limited selection of photographs of Selassie were pretty much all familiar to me; these pictures, though, were unique and of high-quality colour.

Caleb also gave me an Ethiopian coin with the head of Halie Selassie on it. Later, my mother borrowed the coin from me and returned it gold plated and connected to a gold chain as a birthday present.

I spoke to several Rastamen about Selassie being God but never got a satisfactory explanation. I read, but nothing seemed to gel. There were some things about Rastafarian ideology that resonated with me: not eating pork, not drinking alcohol and becoming an "ital dread" (vegetarian) were appealing. Smoking ganja always left a question mark because if it was truly for the "healing of the nations" (a biblical phrase from the book of Revelation), then I did not see why I had to pay for it or why it was illegal. However, Selassie being God? The jury was out on that pivotal doctrine.

There was a song I enjoyed hearing Jah Shaka play by Hugh Mundell called "Africa Must Be Free By 1983". However, whilst I liked the song (or more so the rhythm and bassline), I just could not bring myself to believe, based on the political situation in South Africa at the time (the late 1970s), that it would ever come true, at least not by the year 1983.

When I asked Rastamen about it, they would say there was an error in the calendar and that the current date was incorrect. The mistake they were referring to was approximately four years (depending on which calendar you use). In my mind at the time, this still would not give enough time for there to be a successful political, economic and social shift in Africa.

Although these unresolved questions were not enough in themselves to shake my belief in Rastafarianism, I soon had an encounter that I can only describe as the weakest link in the chain breaking.

CHALLENGES TO MY IDEOLOGY

Chapter 3

> **"The test of first-rate intelligence is the ability to hold two opposed ideas in mind at the same time and still retain the ability to function."**
>
> Francis Scott Key Fitzgerald
> Novelist

My First Meeting with a Seventh-day Adventist

It was winter 1980. Gus was a friend and a Rastaman who worked in the electronics industry repairing audio equipment and was in the second year of the three-year electronics course I wanted to do. Gus was deeply into his music. He was four or five years older than me, so I looked up to him somewhat as a man who knew and understood the deep things of Rastafarianism. We arranged to meet at his house one Sunday when his father was out of the country on holiday.

The plan was to smoke a chalice and listen to Augustus Pablo's music (a hard-core roots-rock-reggae musician). Gus had a lot of interesting books on Rastafarianism and reggae music. I was returning a book I had borrowed from him called *Reggae Bloodlines* and was hoping to borrow another and get a few more profound insights into the Rasta faith.

Within ten minutes of arriving at Gus' house, there was an unexpected knock on the door. It was an old friend of Gus', a guy called Michael Lunan. Michael walked into Gus' bedroom holding a big black Bible in his hand.

From the conversation we had with Michael, it became apparent he had been deeply into roots-rock-reggae and had owned dub plates. In addition, he was closely acquainted with one of the top sounds from yesteryear called Neville Enchanter, a sound that I had heard people much older and more connected than me talk positively about. However, Michael had given all this up and had gotten serious about the religion he was raised in.

I was looking forward to an afternoon of smoking a chalice for the first time and listening to Gus' extensive record collection. However, Michael turning up unexpectedly put a dampener on proceedings, which annoyed me no end. Gus had great respect for him and his religious beliefs, so he did not light up the chalice as it would have offended Michael, and he'd probably have left. I resented his presence.

Soon, the conversation got on to religion. Michael asked a hundred and one questions about Rastafarianism, all of which

Gus and I answered by using one-liners from reggae songs. However, Michael seemed to answer all of our questions by referring directly to the Bible.

Finally, Michael asked the six-million-dollar question: "If Selassie is a reincarnation of Jesus Christ, as you claim, what did he come back to Earth to do? Selassie did not do anything spectacular when he was on Earth." He went on to explain. "Jesus, when he came the first time, came to die on the cross for our sins, and when He comes a second time, it'll all be over."

I did not fully understand the meaning of what he said, but it was said with him referring to the Bible and with deep conviction. I looked to Gus to answer the question. I thought my mentor and friend would be able to give Michael a convincing answer. However, the reply that Gus gave made no sense at all to me and lacked conviction.

Michael said if we wanted to know more, why not come to his church in Hampstead one Saturday. Whilst I resented Michael's presence, I felt that he could be on to something, so I agreed.

We booked 28 February 1981, my seventeenth birthday, a few months away, which fell on a Saturday that year. I had a Saturday job and planned not to work on my birthday, plus it would be easy for me to remember the appointment. So we exchanged numbers and went our different ways.

This chance meeting seemed to be more than a coincidence. Instead of getting deeper into Rastafarianism, I ended up getting a glimpse into Christianity.

Things Seemed Different

During my final year at school, 1980, on the odd occasion I would go out with Moa Anbessa on Wednesday nights to the Four Aces Club in Dalston. I'd travel by bus to Battersea. We'd load up the truck with the equipment, drive to Dalston, unload the truck, cable up the sound, and listen to music all night long. When the club finished at 5.00 a.m. on Thursday, we would reload the truck and drive back to Battersea. Berris would then give me a lift home; I'd shower and then go off to school.

In the summer of 1980, after unsurprisingly getting poor exam results, I applied to college to study electronic engineering. I thought, *I need to start working hard. I need to try to make something of myself.* It was pretty clear to me that the trajectory I was on was not a successful one. My parents were quite liberal and chilled out about many things, but unemployment was not one of them. Consequently, they viewed work as absolutely essential.

I remember being interviewed at college by the head of department, a Welshman called Mr Thompson. The policy was that one of your parents had to attend the interview with you. I distinctly remember my mother and Mr Thompson getting into a debate about unemployment and the chances of young black teenagers getting a job after completing the course.

Mr Thompson, being a Welshman, reassured my mother and expressed that he could sympathise with the situation. However, my mother disagreed and said it was not the same. She stated that the colour of your skin would always create more prejudice than a person's accent.

I was successful in my application and started Carshalton College the following term, September 1980.

One morning, while getting ready to go to college, my younger brother Robert and I were alone in the kitchen. He told me that Mum had said if I got more sleep I would do much better in my exams. That statement encouraged me to go out less frequently because I saw going to college and passing my exams as a way of increasing my chances of getting a job.

Some Rastamen did blue-collar work, others were entrepreneurs who owned and ran their own businesses, but some refused to work. I thought being unemployed deliberately was utterly wrong. They reasoned that paying taxes was supporting Babylon (an oppressive capitalist government). Wilful unemployment went directly against how I was brought up, and I had no respect for such an attitude.

By 1981, I had left school and pretty much left the Moa Anbessa sound system. As a result, I tended to go out much less, but during college my mind was still on sound systems, albeit from a different perspective. I was thinking more along the lines of functioning in a back-office capacity.

The insight I had was that two prominent people built amplifiers for most of the top sound systems. Both were men called Errol, one of whom I'd met when I went to his house with Berris to get one of the amplifiers repaired. My ambition was to learn as much as possible about electronics, get a full-time job and design and build the best amplifiers as a hobby.

After my encounter with Michael Lunan at Gus' house, things never really seemed the same. I began to have serious doubts about critical aspects of the Rastafarian ideology. I reasoned that if Selassie was not God, then many of the lyrics in the songs that I loved were incorrect, smoking weed for spiritual healing was wrong, and the sound systems that promoted the Rastafarian ideology were on the wrong trajectory. It no longer added up in my mind.

On the occasions I went out, it seemed flat, uneventful; the sense of purpose seemed to have evaporated.

Planned Birthday Celebrations Go Sour

My seventeenth birthday, 28 February 1981, finally arrived. Michael, Gus and I had arranged to meet at Gus' house early on Saturday morning to go to church. Gus lived in Sydenham, two to three miles from where I lived in Upper Norwood. Michael's home, in Herne Hill, was about four miles from Sydenham.

Michael's church, however, was an eleven-mile trek across London.

I caught a bus to Gus' house and arrived on time. Michael was accompanied by two of his brothers, Donald and Randal. They drove a small yellow Datsun and also arrived on time, but Gus was nowhere to be seen. We waited outside Gus' house for the best part of an hour, but he did not turn up. I'd stayed in that Friday night so that I could be up and ready to go to church on Saturday morning, but I just knew that Gus had gone to listen to Jah Shaka at Phebes, an all-night club in Stoke Newington, and had not made it home.

From the way they were dressed, cleanly shaven and neatly groomed, it dawned on me that going to church meant going to a formal worship service. I had assumed that because it was a Saturday, the event was some type of informal meeting. I felt that there was no way I was going to church with these three guys on my own, so we waited until it was too late to go to Hampstead. They suggested we go to an Adventist church in Balham instead, which was much closer, but I resisted and gave the excuse that we should go to their church or not at all. They understood, and we all went our separate ways.

I left Gus' and visited Derek Chambers at his house in South Norwood. Everton Bennett was there. I told them it was my birthday, and they agreed to pick me up that evening around the usual time of 10.30 p.m. to go to a blues party in Croydon. A sound from Brixton, Ital Rockers, would be playing there.

Strangely, that night, Derek and Everton did not turn up. I found out the next day that it was because Everton's girlfriend, Germaine Huggins, had gone into labour and given birth, so they spent the night down at Mayday Hospital in Croydon. So both plans for my seventeenth birthday went sour. I did not get to go to church and I did not go to the blues party.

Looking back, my birthday plans turning sour was perhaps one of the best things that could have happened to me. Whilst I was on a trajectory towards discovering the truth, my frame of mind meant that I was not yet ready for the journey towards Christianity. While I was eager to find out the truth, at that point in time I wouldn't have valued it enough to fully accept it. There were still some bitter and sweet experiences I would need to have to be fully prepared for what God had in store for me.

RACIAL TENSIONS

Chapter 4

"...until the colour of a man's skin is of no more significance than the colour of his eyes...everywhere is war."

Haile Selassie
Late Emperor of Ethiopia

An Explosive Atmosphere

In Croydon, where I grew up, the atmosphere was tense. There were periodic encounters between right-wing racists and young black people such as me. That, coupled with the infamous SUS ("suspected person") law, which gave the police the legal right to arrest a person who they thought was loitering with intent to commit an arrestable offence, caused tension in the late 1970s. The way certain factions of the Metropolitan Police implemented the SUS law was to arrest any young black person they felt was thinking of committing a crime, be it if you were about to board a bus and got what they considered too close to someone or just hanging out on a street corner.

I had some close encounters with racists thugs, which could have ended up with me being hospitalised. I also had several close encounters with the police, which fortunately did not end up with me going to court. Unfortunately, other black youths were not so fortunate and, when stopped for SUS, ended up in court and were sentenced to time in a youth detention centre.

On one occasion I, along with several other black and white guys from school, was walking down the street during the school lunch break when a few police cars pulled up beside us. Officers jumped out of the cars and began to question us. After a few minutes, the white pupils were all dismissed while the black pupils were held.

I remember the policeman who searched me. One of his colleagues stood by and watched everything; his badge number was Z656. The policeman who searched me took away my afro comb and tried to get me to agree that it was an offensive weapon; he took my lip salve and strongly suggested that it was lipstick and that I was a "poof" (an offensive term for homosexuals). Each suggestion and accusation was accompanied by the policeman firmly pushing his finger in my chest. I refused to retaliate. We were eventually let go.

On other occasions, my friends and I would be pushed up against the wall, searched and questioned about what we were doing and asked where we were going. But, as I said, not all encounters had such a peaceful end. It was not uncommon to hear of resistance ending in arrests, court appearances and, on some occasions, incarceration.

The actions of the police, met with pushback from the youth, contributed to an atmosphere that was dense with hostility—the perfect breeding ground for the trouble to come.

In April 1981, riots broke out in Brixton between the police and the black community, five miles from where I lived in Norwood/Croydon. There are different theories as to what sparked the riots. A government report concluded that they were the result of social and economic problems. However, many would say that police provocation triggered the incidents, resulting in looting, damage to buildings, and injuries.

Close Shave 1

One Saturday night, in early May 1981, I was walking home up South Norwood Hill and was jumped by three white guys. I remember hearing footsteps behind me; I stopped and turned around but did not see anyone; then, suddenly, I was dragged to the ground. I managed to wrestle myself free quickly. They all jumped back (luckily, they did not have the sense to surround me).

I sized them up and was sure that I would be able to take them on. One of them looked straight at me and said, "Come on, you bleep bleep bleep." Looking at them, I felt if any of them had a knife, I would be in real trouble. I did not have a knife. My father forbade me from taking one out at night.

The three white guys stood on the pavement between me and the way I needed to go. I happened to be wearing trainers, so I quickly darted into the road among the traffic and ran in the direction of my home. Fortunately for me, I did not get hit by a car.

A white couple saw the incident, pulled over and offered me a lift home, which was five minutes' drive away. When I got home, I told my dad. We immediately jumped in his car and went looking for the three white guys, but they were nowhere to be seen.

Murder Outside the Wilton Arms Pub

Sunday night, 31 May 1981, a group of us were hanging out in a car park in Croydon. When we left and began to walk home, I asked my friends if there would be anything happening on Monday night. No one replied.

I went to college Monday morning, 1 June 1981, came home in the evening, did my assignments and went to bed early. The next day, I learnt that there was a murder in Thornton Heath outside the Wilton Arms Pub. The catalyst was a National Front (NF) meeting being held in the pub that night.

The word on the street was that the NF had ambitions to set up a headquarters in Thornton Heath, but unfortunately the Monday night that the meeting was held turned into a riot, resulting in one of the most senseless, tragic, and cowardly murders known in Croydon: the murder of an innocent disabled white guy who was pulled off his motorbike and killed.

As I reflect on the countless numbers of tragic and senseless racial killings and murders worldwide, mainly in the UK and the United States, I think of the words of the speech Emperor Haile Selassie made to the United Nations General Assembly on 4 October 1963. These words formed the basis of the song sung by Bob Marley entitled "War". The lyrics to the first few verses are:

Until the philosophy which hold one race

superior

and another

inferior

is finally

and permanently

discredited

and abandoned

everywhere is war

Me say war.

That until there no longer

first-class and second-class citizens of any

nation

Until the colour of a man's skin is of no more

significance than the colour of his eyes

Me say war

That until the basic human rights

are equally guaranteed to all

Without regard to race

Dis a war

If it were possible for humanity to adopt the sentiments of the speech or song, then I'm sure there would be less racial tension in the world. Or better still, embrace the words of Jesus:

"But I say unto you, love your enemies, bless them that curse you, do good to them that hate you, and pray for them that despitefully use you and persecute you."

Matthew 5:44

Putting into practice Jesus' teaching would eradicate racism and all other types of prejudice along with the accompanying senseless violence and killings.

A Sprained Ankle That Kept Me Safe

Following on from the murder by the Wilton Arms Pub, the NF organised a march the following weekend through Croydon. Naturally, word got around, and there were plans to confront and break the rally up.

To get to college, I would catch the 196 bus from my home in Upper Norwood to Norwood Junction train station, a fifteen-minute journey. Then, as the Routemaster bus pulled up outside the station, I would jump off the opening at the back of the bus before it had fully stopped and run like mad through the gates and down the steps to get to the platform where my train would arrive.

Olrick Nicholl, a school and college friend, caught the same train. He lived down the road from the station so was not dependent, as I was, on a bus to get to the train station on time. We had an agreement that if the bus was running late and he saw me coming, he would hold open the train door to give me a few extra seconds to make it.

This particular Friday morning, the bus was running a fraction late. When it pulled up outside the station, I jumped off before it came to a stop and ran for the steps. I could see my train was just pulling up to the platform. Two little kids jumped out in front of me, doing star jumps. I swerved to avoid knocking them down but slipped! I went tumbling down the steps.

Immediately, I sprang up and went to grab my bag, only to collapse in dreadful pain. My ankle!

I lay on the ground, screaming in agony. The commuters just walked past me. No one stopped to ask, "Are you OK?" Olrick had delayed the train as long as possible and then travelled off to college, not knowing my predicament. I felt helpless and, at the same time, incensed that a group of people would just walk past me in broad daylight and not offer so much as a helping hand when I was clearly in need of assistance.

The wave of commuters who came off the train that had just pulled up dispersed, but eventually an old Indian man stopped and said he would get me help. He went and got this six-foot-tall, four-foot-wide, black train guard who picked me up like a baby and carried me into the office. I thanked the Indian man with all my heart. He replied, "It's OK. We're brothers."

The guard put my foot in a bucket of cold water to bring the swelling down. After a while, I left and caught a bus back home.

Usually, it took me less than five minutes to walk home from my local bus stop. However, this particular day, it took over twenty minutes to hobble halfway. Fortunately, my next-door neighbour, Val, saw me as she drove past. She stopped and gave me a lift the rest of the way home.

My sprained ankle meant that I could barely limp from one room to the next, let alone go out to oppose the NF over the weekend. When my school friends came knocking for me, they had a sports bag full of weapons to take to the march. I bailed out, showing them my swollen ankle. They went off to do battle without me.

Close Shave 2

A month or so after the murder by the Wilton Arms pub, I, along with a large number of people from Croydon, was at a nightclub in Clapham Junction. At 11.00 p.m., when the club closed, we all left and got a train bound for West Croydon. Most of us were going to the cinema in Croydon to watch all-night Kung Fu films or to Rainbow, the nightclub in East Croydon. I decided to get off at Thornton Heath, a few stops before Croydon, and walk home from there.

I came out of the station alone and looked down the road toward the Wilton Arms. Several white guys who looked like skinheads were walking towards me but were a little way off. I was wearing dress shoes, as opposed to my trainers, so I could not run. However, they were between me and the direction I wanted to go.

At the junction of Parchmore Road and Thornton Heath High Street, a clock tower with a bushy central reservation divided Parchmore Road vertically. Opposite the central reservation was a minicab station. I quickly went to hide in the sparse bushes.

My heart was pounding and I was hyperventilating with fear. What should I do next? At that moment, a cab pulled up. I felt relieved at the possibility of getting out of my predicament unscathed. I crawled on all fours, like a dog, across the road to keep out of sight, opened the back door of the cab, got in, crouched down low so I would not be seen and asked the driver to take me home to Upper Norwood (a few miles away). The cab driver was concerned that I might not pay him and do a runner. It was not uncommon for young black guys to not only refuse to pay but to also rob cab drivers. I said to him, "Please, please drive quickly. I promise I'll pay you—I won't do a runner. You've got to drive quickly … please."

I crouched down in the back seat as he drove around the clock tower; I gingerly peered out the window and saw the skinheads looking in the bushes. Then, feeling a great sense of relief, I sat up in the car properly, my heartbeat gradually returned to normal, and I thought, *That was another close shave….*

A Cause for Deep Reflection

On the 18 June 1981, when I was seventeen, I went to a dance in Brixton Town Hall. Traditionally, town hall dances would start around 7.00 or 7.30 p.m. and end roughly at 10.30 or 11.00 p.m. After that, it would be nightclubs or parties till 6.00 a.m. In the town hall, I bumped into Brenda, a girl who used to live down the road from me.

About five years prior, when Brenda and I were about twelve years old, my little sister, Lisa, who would have been about eight, ran up the street into our home, through the open front door, screaming that Brenda was going to beat her up. Hearing the commotion, I began to walk toward the front door, ready to give Brenda a piece of my mind.

Neither Brenda nor I realised that Lisa had flipped the latch on the front door, locking it shut as she ran into the house. The door was usually unlocked and the kids in the street would push the door open and walk in and out pretty much as they pleased.

As I approached the door, Brenda, being angry, pushed the six-foot-tall door that had a five-foot-tall, low budget council (local government) fitted glass pane. Unfortunately, the impact of Brenda's push caused the glass to explode! It shot out all along the passageway through to the kitchen.

I was about three to four feet from the front door when this happened. The glass went all over me and cut open my side. Unfortunately, the glass also went all over Brenda, who was wearing a halter neck top. It cut her chest, shoulders and upper arm region. Our dads rushed us to Mayday Hospital. I received five stitches and was left with an ugly scar on the side of my waist. Brenda received twenty stitches in visible areas of her body, so I can only imagine that her scarring would have been significantly uglier.

Previous to this incident, Brenda and I would disagree and argue about everything and anything. Now we ignored each other. Our families also fell out over the incident, shortly after Brenda's family moved away from Ravensdale Gardens.

When I met Brenda that night in Brixton Town Hall, I did not want her to see me smoking weed. I could not risk her mentioning to my parents what I was up to as a way of getting even, should she bump into them or anyone else who lived on the street.

We briefly spoke. She said that after Brixton Town Hall, she was going to a party in New Cross and wanted me to come along with her—probably so we could split the cab fare home. I was not interested because I did not relish spending the night not smoking. I had nowhere else to go after the town hall dance, so I went home.

The following day, news broke of the tragic fire at a party in New Cross where several people were burned to death.

Traditionally I'd sleep in late on a Sunday morning after being out on a Saturday night. When my parents heard the news of the fire, they immediately checked to see that I was safely in bed sleeping.

I did not know if the party Brenda invited me to was the same one that went up in flames. However, two years after the incident, I bumped into her and she was not sure if it was the same party.

While being out and about, I had come under various types of risks and threats: a chisel put to my throat while in a dance in Wandsworth Town Hall, a policeman walking past me while I smoked a spliff outside a club in Notting Hill, and clubs being raided. However, the threat of receiving second or third-degree burns or being burnt alive while struggling to get out of a crowded venue was a risk I had never had to consider when going out to enjoy myself.

A few weeks after the fire, while out at a club in Clapham Junction, I heard a MC reciting lyrics that suggested the New Cross fire was deliberately started to kill the occupants of the party. Some of the lyrics suggested that Rastamen were invincible.

As the MC sang away, I thought the claim of being invincible was absurd! The fire was no respecter of persons. The reality of death came home to me and caused me to reflect on the Rastafarian ideology deeply.

EDUCATION AND EMPLOYMENT

Chapter 5

> **"There can be no progress, no achievement, without sacrifice, and a man's worldly success will be in the measure that he sacrifices."**
>
> James Allen
> Author

Studying at Carshalton College

I lived in Upper Norwood, and South London College was in West Norwood, a ten-to-fifteen-minute bus ride down the road from where I lived. Instead of applying to study at South London College, I chose to spend the best part of an hour travelling out of London to Carshalton College because it was farther away from the whole reggae nightlife scene.

I felt that I had to focus and avoid as many distractions as possible. I had allowed myself to be distracted during my last two years at school and consequently left school with no real qualifications. I did not want to repeat the same mistake.

At Carshalton College, I learnt how to study. Every Friday we had a test. Every Friday, I scored between 50% and 60%. Most of the class scored between 80% and 100%.

After one such test, I stayed behind in my seat when the class was dismissed. I was holding my head in my hands, feeling quite low.

The lecturer, Mr Ken Philips, approached me and asked, "What's the matter, Mr Morrison?"

"I don't get it, sir. Every week I spend a lot of time studying for the test, but I'm just not getting a high score like everyone else," I replied.

He handed me a copy of the test paper and said, "It's up to you... You can go to the library and photocopy it, go over the questions you got wrong and read about that topic in your textbook and other books in the library; then, after you've done that go over the questions again."

I took the paper out of his hand.

"I want the paper back before you go home!"

This was the first time that someone had given me an idea of how to study. I often heard phrases like, "Study your books," and "Study hard—make sure you do well at school," but no one had shown me how.

The one problem with Mr Philips' suggestion was that I did not have enough money to photocopy the whole paper, buy lunch and catch a bus and train home. If I copied the paper, I'd be broke. Slipping through the train station gates without paying was risky but doable. However, going without lunch was going to be tough. I thought about it and decided to spend my train fare and lunch money on photocopying the paper.

One might argue that Mr Philips should have photocopied the paper on the staff photocopier machine and given it to me free of charge. But making me pay for the photocopying was probably the best thing he could have done because it meant that I valued the paper. It had cost me my lunch and, as a result, I made sure that I capitalised as much as possible on the opportunity.

From that point on, my Friday test scores improved until I eventually was up there, scoring 80% and 90% each week. Finally, in the summer of 1981, I passed my City & Guilds exams with good grades. It was my first taste of academic success.

Following Advice Paid Off

In 1981, there was a recession, and it was estimated that approximately 10% of the workforce (2.5 million people) were unemployed—the highest it had been for fifty years. For me, the exams were over; however, the common complaint in my college class was, "What's the use of continuing to study if there are no jobs?" but in my house, unemployment was not acceptable.

While I was at school, my parents made sure that I had a midweek paper round. When I complained that I did not earn enough money from doing it, they arranged for my older brother, Leslie, to fix me up with a job at the Queens Hotel in Crystal Palace. Leslie was a drinking buddy of one of the owners of the hotel. Nevertheless, after attending college for a year, I was determined to get a job in the field I studied, despite the recession.

Mr Philips' response to the complaints from his students regarding the lack of employment opportunities was to tell us to pick up the Yellow Pages (a telephone directory) and call or write to all the electronic companies in the area. He even gave us an outline of the pitch to use when calling, telling us to outline to a potential employer the skills we had learnt, the equipment we could use and the value we could give. On reflection, I'm sure that most of the students thought Mr Philips was crazy, but I had taken his advice before and it had paid off, so I took his advice again.

I clearly remember one Friday morning, sitting down at home with the Yellow Pages in one hand and the telephone in the other. In the '80s, there was no internet, no online job boards, no mobile phones and no LinkedIn. By today's standards, job seeking was hard work. I started calling companies.

The third or fourth company I called was Clifford & Snell, an electronics company in Purley Way, Croydon. Immediately, I was put through to a manager, a man called Mr Pearson. I gave my elevator pitch, just as Mr Philips had outlined, and to my surprise, Mr Pearson asked if I could come down straight away for an interview!

I ran up the stairs, got changed, and my mum dropped me off at the company. The interview lasted about twenty-five minutes. I remember someone came into the interview with a test paper for me to take, but Mr Pearson said it was not needed because I had scored a distinction on one of my exams. So I was offered the job on the spot.

Mr Pearson queried if I had to go back to college on Monday or if I'd be free to start work. I assured him that even though there were still classes, the exams were over, so it would be okay for me to start work first thing Monday morning. When I shared the good news with my parents, their faces beamed; they could not have been happier and prouder of me.

I phoned Carshalton College and left a message for Mr Philips explaining that I would not be returning to college until next term because I had got a job. He announced it to the class the same Friday just before giving out the test papers. Later on, I heard that he had announced it with glee because someone had followed his advice and it had worked out.

So, I was the first person out of a class of about thirty to leave college with a job. I found it incredibly miraculous that I, who was not the brightest person in the class, should get a job— particularly in the middle of a recession. I pondered this deeply and concluded that it must be the hand of God.

There was something inside me that had always said there was a God in Heaven. I just did not know anything about Him. By this time, I had pretty much concluded that Selassie was not God and that Rastafarianism, whilst having good intentions and some valuable teachings, was not the absolute truth. But one thing is for sure; despite being raised by parents who were atheist/agnostic, I always knew there was a God in Heaven.

When I was ten or eleven, I used to recite the first verse of the song "A Child's Prayer" by the soul group Hot Chocolate. Each night, I lay in bed believing with all my childish heart that there was a God somewhere in Heaven above who heard my prayer. The first verse of the song is:

Say a little prayer, baby, before you go to sleep

Say a little prayer and give the Lord thy soul to

keep

Say a little prayer, darlin'

For all the people in the world

That their hearts will be happy, filled with joy.

So, believing that God in Heaven had intervened in my life and given me a job, I was encouraged to find out more about Him.

Michael had phoned me a few times since our abandoned trip to his church back in February 1981, but I just kind of brushed him off. But now (around June/July) I believed that God had helped me out and I wanted to find out more. Michael seemed like a genuine and friendly guy who could give me a little insight.

THE SEVENTH-DAY ADVENTIST CHURCH

Chapter 6

> **"If you find a perfect church
> don't join it: you'd spoil it."**
>
> Billy Graham
> Evangelist

My First Visit to a Seventh-day Adventist Church

At Clifford & Snell, I met a Christian fellow and shared with him my conviction that God had opened the door for me to get this job. One Wednesday night, we got into a deep and heartfelt conversation. I guess I had bottled up my emotions for years. I cried and told him that my biological mother had just vanished without even saying goodbye and I had not seen her for years and did not know where she was. He said to me words that I've never forgotten:

"If you give your life to Jesus, everything will be alright."

He prayed for me and I got the sense that everything was going to be alright. I had arranged to meet Michael at his house the next day, and I had another deep conversation. He invited me to church that Saturday. I accepted the offer.

Saturday came and I met Michael at his house. Michael's younger brother, Patrick, went to get their dad's 7 Series BMW car from the garage. I remember having negative feelings because they had a big house, a top-quality car and were dressed in suits and ties. I thought to myself, *What do these people know about hard work, injustice and oppression?* (The key themes of roots-rock-reggae.) However, as I walked out of the house, two things happened that dispelled my negative feelings.

The first was that Michael's father, Mr Herman Lunan, met me as I was about to go out of the front door. He greeted me with a smile, shook my hand. His huge hand engulfed mine. It was as rough as coarse sandpaper, yet he held my hand with a firm but gentle grip and said, "Peace."

The second followed immediately after. As he moved out of the way, I saw a plaque on the wall that said, "The Lord Giveth, the Government Taketh Away." It made me smile inside, and any resentment I had faded away.

When we arrived at church, two things held my attention: the Sabbath school discussion group and the group that sang.

The Sabbath School Discussion Group

The Sabbath school discussion group is akin to a book club. The Seventh-day Adventist Church studies a topic each quarter from a booklet known as a quarterly. Each calendar quarter is split into thirteen weekly lessons, and each lesson has a short daily reading with a few questions and corresponding Bible texts to look up for the answer.

When I arrived at Michael's church, I was given a quarterly. That particular quarterly was entitled "This We Believe: the fundamental doctrines of the Seventh-day Adventist Church based on the Bible." I took well to the quarterly because reading it reminded me of doing comprehension at school, which I enjoyed.

As I sat in the discussion group, I was so impressed that everybody knew, understood, and could explain their point of view from the Bible while being open and respectful of the opinion of others. The thing that amazed me the most was that the whole church was involved, irrespective of age. When I queried why middle-aged and senior citizens were involved in Sabbath school classes, Randal said, "When it comes to the Bible, you never stop learning." It seemed like the church was set up for lifelong learning.

The Group That Sang

After Sabbath school, there was a fifteen-minute interlude followed by the worship service. A group called the Escoffery Sisters sang. I was accustomed to listening to a few UK female reggae groups, like Fifteen, Sixteen and Seventeen, or solo artists like Janet Kay, but the Escoffery Sisters' vocals were far superior; their harmony and melody sounded perfect and they sang with a real depth of meaning.

What Do We Have in Common?

After church, Michael's mother invited me to stay for lunch. I accepted the invitation but did not want to stay. I remember saying to Michael, away from everybody else's earshot, "I think I'll go home."

"Why?" Michael asked.

"I don't fancy staying."

"Come on," he said.

He gently yet persistently pleaded until I finally admitted the real reason I didn't want to stay.

"I don't eat pork."

I'll never forget the slight frown that came over his face as he said, "Neither do we."

I later found out that Seventh-day Adventists refrain from eating pork and other unclean meats as outlined in the Bible and abstain from drinking alcohol and smoking cigarettes. Additionally, they encourage a plant-based/vegan or vegetarian diet. All of these things resonated with me as they were in harmony with what Rastafarianism taught and what I had been practising since I was thirteen.

The Seventh-day Adventist church bases all of its teachings on what the Bible says, and so I decided to do some research about the Bible itself. I came to appreciate that the Bible had been translated from the original Greek and Hebrew to English at different points in history. For example, the English language changed from Shakespearean to what we know as modern English over the centuries. Also, over time, scholars' understanding of the original languages increased and enabled them to use more precise words in translations. I also learnt that there were different types of translations, e.g. word for word, sentence for sentence or phrase for phrase.

However, the clincher for me was the findings of the Dead Sea Scrolls in the 1940s/'50s, which confirmed that the King James Version of the Bible we have in our hands today is a trustworthy translation of the original manuscripts. In my research, I also discovered that the books of the Apocrypha were pretty much history books written in the four hundred years between the writing of the Old and New Testaments of the Bible. They were not hidden and were available if I wanted to get a copy of them.

Sunday or Saturday

On the occasions that I went to church as a child, it was always on a Sunday. This was either with my sister as part of her Girls' Brigade or for a Boys' Brigade parade.

Back in the 1970s, many shops closed on Sunday as it was considered a holy day, a day of rest, a day not to do business. I remember seeing minibuses full of people driving to church on Sundays, so the whole idea of going to church on a Saturday seemed counterintuitive. I studied with Michael the validity of the Ten Commandments, something I had never heard of.

The Ten Commandments state that the seventh day of the week is the Sabbath. So I researched which day was the seventh day, and, to my surprise, I discovered Sunday was the first day of the week, making Saturday the seventh. The irony of the whole matter is that the only commandment that has been forgotten is the one that starts with "remember".

It took me a while to come to terms with this newly found fact. I was surprised that the true identity of the day of rest had been hidden. Finally, I decided to keep the biblical Sabbath day holy (a twenty-four-hour period from sunset Friday to sunset Saturday). During this time, no secular work or business is carried out. It is a day of rest, a chance to recharge your batteries.

Later on in life, I discovered that Sabbath-keeping had been scientifically proven to contribute to an increased life expectancy.

An Ideal Mentor

Michael and Randel introduced me to Robert Sango, who was a friend of theirs. Robert was twelve years my senior; however, we became good friends because of our similar backgrounds. We often exchanged experiences and opinions on everything from music and politics to comparing how our mothers managed us as children. Both of our mothers smoked and we were both concerned about their health. One evening, I went around to Robert's house. We were in his living room; I said, "What's up, Robert?"

"She's given up."

"What?"

"She's kicked the habit—my mum has stopped smoking!"

Robert sat in his chair with a smile on his face, gently nodding, and in a low-key voice, said, "I'm telling you, man, she's given up the cigarettes!"

I don't think I'd ever seen him so happy.

Robert would take me to a few specialist book shops introducing me to a range of authors and Bible study tools. Afterwards, he'd say to me, "You must invest in books and create your own university." Then, pointing at his forehead, he'd continue, "What you put up here no one can take away from you."

Robert had a wealth of knowledge second to none, yet he had an unassuming nature.

At times we would spend all night studying, reading and discussing the scriptures. He encouraged me to dig deep and get a thorough understanding of topics, especially the prophecies of Daniel and Revelations.

He hosted a Bible study group that met once a week and he would encourage everyone to do their independent research and come prepared, especially if it was their turn to lead out in the discussion.

Robert was ahead of me in the journey of life; I regarded him as a big brother. He would give me tips about navigating through some challenges that lay ahead of me.

Often, we'd be walking down the street and see either a homeless person or, at night, a drunk in the gutter, and he'd say, "There go I but for the grace of God."

Unfortunately, Robert unexpectedly passed away in 2018. His funeral was held in the Brixton Seventh-day Adventist Church. His younger brother, Steven Sango, delivered a moving eulogy that evoked every emotion possible and helped those present to reflect and celebrate Robert's life.

Robert's Eulogy

For those of you that don't know me, I'm Robert's brother, Steven, and although many of you know him as Robert, he's always been my brother Bobby, so if you don't mind, I'll refer to him in familiar terms.

I'd like to begin by thanking you all on behalf of myself and my family for joining us today. Bobby would be honoured, as we are, by your presence here.

I would definitely say there were two phases in Bobby's life. The before Christ, which I'll outline for you first.

Bobby was born on 9 December 1952, sixteen months before me, and we grew up close to this church in Brixton. As two mixed-race kids growing up in Brixton in the late fifties and early sixties, we had fun, played football and made mischief, but sometimes we encountered prejudice and hostility, both at school and on the streets.

It may surprise some of Bobby's church friends to know that as a young boy, he was a fierce fighter and was not one to take insults lightly or suffer fools gladly. He took on the big brother role as my protector and took care of me while I was young and took *'care'* of people who bullied me at school.

As a young man, he began washing cars on a Saturday to earn money so he could indulge in his passion for buying records and clothes and as soon as he was old enough he began going to clubs to wear his new clothes and hear the music he loved.

He would come home and tell me all about the tunes he'd heard and the girls he'd chatted to and danced with.

This continued through his teenage years, him going out regularly with my cousins John, Jimmy Thomas, Brownie and the rest of their gang until a chance meeting when he was around twenty years old led to his initial interest in the church.

His interest in the church quickly moved from curiosity to being preoccupied with Bible studies and reading and learning the scriptures. He then began attending church on a regular basis.

Then one day he told me what to me was bombshell news!

"Steve, I've become a Seventh-day Adventist," said Bobby.

"What? What does that mean?" I replied.

"It means I'll be going to church and Bible studies regularly and I'm gonna be baptised."

"What you saying? You're Bobby, the tough guy; you're not gonna go to church every week and get baptised. Let's have a cigarette and talk about this."

"I don't smoke cigarettes anymore," said Bobby.

"Whaaat! Let's smoke one of those other things you smoke then and have a *deep* talk about it," I replied.

"Don't do that anymore either."

"A drink and a chat then?"

"Nah, given up drink too!"

"Jesus!" I exclaimed.

"Exactly!" Bobby replied.

And so it was! Bobby had now entered the second phase of his life. He was now a Seventh-day Adventist, no more drinking or smoking of any kind.

He attended church every week and read book after book to increase his knowledge. He was eventually baptised at Hampstead Church in 1973.

He continued attending church and Bible studies whilst working as a car panel beater and sprayer, a trade he continued his whole working life.

He loved an old banger!

He'd buy them damaged and repair and spray them and sell them on.

Bobby met Marie in 1982; they fell in love and were married in 1984. Marie had a six-month-old daughter Rene who Bobby loved and brought up as his own. Their daughter Sarah was born in 1985.

He integrated his children into the church at an early age and they enjoyed many family holidays at church conventions and activity weeks at seaside resorts.

His favourite holidays were to Jamaica with the girls when they were older, a big family holiday to Portugal and his trip to Jamaica by himself.

Bobby was now a man of simpler pleasures and enjoyed his cycling and teaching the girls how to cook lentil soup, bake bread and make herbal teas. He would also enjoy taking them to Dulwich Park to feed the ducks and shake the trees till the apples dropped off. He would also take a boomerang to the park and teach the girls to throw it. I'm reliably informed that it never, ever came back!

The girls grew to be intelligent, strong, ambitious women and he was immensely proud of them; proud that Rene was the first university graduate in our family and proud that Sarah reached the top of her field in Afro-Caribbean hairdressing and goes all around the world to do hair at fashion shows.

He was blessed with two precious grandchildren, Shaheem born in 2005 and Monaei in 2011, whom he adored and doted on.

Bobby was my hero, a man who faced adversity on a daily basis and never complained. Although affected by epilepsy for most of his life, which caused him to have severe fits and seizures, he never got angry or said, "Why me?"

If I'd heard he'd been ill I'd ring him and he'd just say, "I'm alright, mate, God is good."

I'm sure the strength he gained from his beliefs played a big part in him being able to deal with his illness.

I'm thankful to Bobby's church friends for the love and support and friendship they always gave him. I'm grateful that the church undoubtedly changed his life for the better and the fiery young man grew into a calm, gentle, beautiful soul.

I'm gonna miss you, Bobby, we all are, but the memories I have of you will never fade. You were so dearly loved by us all.

Rest in Peace. Love lives on and God is Good!

Thank you.

by Steven Sango

VALIDATION

Chapter 7

> **"I believe that everything happens for a reason, but I think it's important to seek out that reason; that's how we learn."**
>
> Drew Barrymore
> Actress

Validations of my decision

After my first visit to Hampstead Seventh-day Adventist Church, I decided to attend each week, leaving home early each Saturday morning. Once a week, Michael would come to my house and give me Bible studies. We spent a few weeks covering questions that I had and then began to study the fundamental teachings of the Seventh-day Adventist Christian faith.

I had a paperback Bible that my biological mother had given me, so I began to read it with vigour for the first time in my life. However, I admired the black leather Bibles that I saw people in the church with.

Michael was a connoisseur of different types and versions of Bibles. I liked the King James Thompson Chain-Reference Bible because it contained numerous fascinating historical, archaeological and biblical topics in the appendix. It also had a chain-reference numbering system that enabled you to study quickly but thoroughly any biblical topic. Michael introduced me to Roger, a man who sold Bibles and religious books for a living.

I remember one night going to Roger's flat deep in the heart of an estate in Brixton to purchase the Bible. Typically, these inner-city housing estates were four to five stories high and consisted of long rows of flats that were all identical with balconies that you could look over and see who was coming. The rows of flats were positioned in such a way as to create a central courtyard where children would play in the day and teenagers would hang out during the night. The outside decor often appeared run down due to a lack of government funding. The environment reminded me of the type of flats where I used to go to blues parties or the type of places I'd go to buy weed, but this time I was buying what I considered a much more precious commodity, a Bible.

Roger showed me several different books and different types of Bibles, but I told him that I was only interested in the Thompson Chain-Reference, which I purchased and began reading as soon as I got home.

I systematically worked my way through the four gospels: Matthew, Mark, Luke and John. Each one gave an account of the life of Jesus from a slightly different perspective. As I read, it would seem as if I was transported to the actual scenes I was reading about; other times, it was like flashes of light would illuminate my mind as I understood what Jesus was saying. It was different from the sensation I felt when the penny would finally drop after studying an electronics book or understanding a complex concept. It was also completely different from the buzz I got from smoking a spliff while listening to inspirational reggae music.

My personal Bible study, alongside studying the lesson quarterly and studying the Bible with Michael, helped me grasp the rudimentary aspects of what is known as The Great Controversy, the battle between Christ and Satan over the human race.

As I prayed and studied, I recognised a change coming over me for the better. Violent thoughts that I had always disliked having gradually became less intense. I felt calmer and less anxious. My language became more considerate and respectful and I looked at people with a more opened mind. These experiences convinced me to give my life to Jesus, to allow Him to be my master—just like the lord of the manor is master over his servants. I wanted to permit Jesus to shape my character to be like His, just like a coach develops a young promising athlete. Furthermore, I wanted to surrender my will to Jesus', just like one wrestler surrendering to another when put in a hold they cannot escape.

I decided to follow Jesus and commit my life to Him irrespective of the opinion of family or friends. However, my decision was just the beginning of my Christian journey. There were several coincidental experiences that validated my decision and several battles that threatened to discourage me.

The French Bible

I was sitting in Hampstead Church one Saturday afternoon after service contemplating the whole idea of going to a dance hall or nightclub. While I believed that I was on the right pathway, I also was fighting ingrained habits of a lifetime (albeit at only seventeen). I enjoyed studying the Bible and, at last, was learning so much—it was like my eyes were opened.

As mentioned, Rastafarians taught that the Bible could not be understood but now here I was understanding different subjects, even whole passages. I would read the scriptures every morning and for two to three hours every evening. I was not an avid reader at school, so I had to work hard at it, but my passion and desire to understand outweighed any academic inabilities I had.

I applied the same method that I'd learnt at college from Mr Philips: if I didn't understand something, I'd focus on it, read it in different versions and, of course, I prayed for understanding before I started reading. The more I read the easier it became. I ensured I had a few different versions of the Bible that I used for cross-referencing. I also used a dictionary a lot and invested in a few Bible commentaries.

As I sat in church and continued to contemplate, wondering if it would be wrong to go out that night, it was like an inner voice said to me, *"If you return to your former lifestyle, reading the Bible will be like reading French."*

Back at school, we had been given the option of dropping certain subjects at age thirteen. For me, it was a no-brainer: I immediately dropped French. It did not make sense to me; I did not like it, and I found it confusing.

I ignored the inner voice, stretched over, and picked up an attractive-looking Bible that someone had left in the pews. I opened it up, and to my astonishment, it was all in French! Someone had left a French Bible in church. That was enough to let me know that my former lifestyle and the current path I was walking on would not and could not go together. It was either one or the other. I was amazed that the French Bible was at arm's length from where I was sitting at the same time that the thought ran through my mind.

The Spider I Could Not Kill

Errol Spence was a friend of mine. He was a Rastaman and lived in the inner city. We were roughly the same age and had spent many hours reasoning and discussing spiritual things. I still kept in touch with him for quite a while after I started going to church, but we eventually drifted apart.

I visited him one day to share what I had learnt at church, as I did with all my friends. I knocked on the door of his Wandsworth flat and waited for him to answer.

At the time, I was going through a phase of wondering whether God was all-powerful. I had my back to the flat's front door and had my arms on the railings opposite. Looking down the steps, I saw a spider crawling around at the bottom of the railings. In my mind, I said to myself and God, *I'll prove that you are not all-powerful by stamping on and killing this spider—and you can't stop me.*

Just as I lifted my foot, Errol answered the door in his typical loud way, startling me with the words, "How are you doing?"

I immediately turned around, forgetting the spider, and gave the loud response, "I'm OK." I went into his flat.

There we were, two young black philosophers reasoning about the social and economic state of different classes in Britain, the paradigm shift needed to bring about equality among all nations and races and the reality of the second coming of Christ.

After a few hours, I decided to head back home. When I opened the front door to leave, I was astonished to see the spider still crawling around. I felt that the timing of Errol's interruption in sync with my thoughts of stamping on the spider could not have been better timed if it had been choreographed.

Smoking Weed: Right or Wrong, Good or Bad?

Back at school (1980), when I was sixteen years old, there was an English lesson where the teacher turned up late and we were all messing around and talking about the types of things schoolboys speak about.

The subject drifted onto music and the usual debate about which music was the best cropped up. In those days, teenagers fell into one of three different music camps: reggae, soul or heavy rock. People began to ask one another what type of music and which artists and bands they liked.

I clearly remember someone asking Morris Wright what type of music he liked. Morris replied, "Country and western." Everyone, including me, burst out laughing—we laughed at him scornfully. I recall laughing so much that my stomach hurt and my jaw ached.

As I laughed, I gazed at Morris, who sat at his desk unperturbed by the whole situation. Then I thought, *Why did you say country and western? You knew what would happen. Why not just say reggae or soul and avoid being laughed at?*

Back to 1981, I was travelling home from work one Friday on a 68 bus, contemplating why it was or was not wrong to smoke cannabis. Rastafarians taught that smoking weed was supported in the scriptures, which I discovered was not the case.

As I got off the bus, I bumped into Morris. I had not seen him since we left school the previous year, but for some unknown reason, in a split second, a flood of memories came back to me about him. I never recalled seeing Morris in nightclubs or at parties; I had no recollection of him being in the headmaster's office with the usual suspects when we were in trouble, and I didn't remember him getting into fights. Instead, Morris seemed to be an upright type of guy, and, of course, he humbly spoke his mind, irrespective of the consequences. I felt so impressed that he must be a Seventh-day Adventist, so I asked him if he was. He said yes, and we began to talk.

I told him of my spiritual journey and asked him about the rights and wrongs of smoking weed. From a biblical point of view, Morris explained that the body is the temple of God and that we ought not to eat or drink anything that would cause damage to our bodies. I appreciated his explanation and felt fortunate that I had bumped into him as I debated the pros and cons of smoking weed.

Over the subsequent weeks, I double-checked everything he said but was still wrestling in my mind whether smoking weed was harmful.

The Hippies Settled It All

After the afternoon programme had finished, I left church one Saturday night and walked a few yards down the road to Chalk Farm tube station to travel home.

As I was waiting on the platform for the tube (underground train) to come, I reasoned that because smoking weed made me feel relaxed, happy and pleasant, then it must be okay. I tried to justify my thinking by telling myself that it was a natural herb used for medicinal purposes. Though, I hadn't entirely settled the matter for myself, and despite the desire to smoke a spliff now and again, I never gave in to my feelings.

I boarded the tube and took a seat contemplating the pros and cons of smoking cannabis. The next stop was Camden Town. A host of commuters boarded the train, among them a guy and a girl; both hippies took their seats opposite me.

There was something about the way hippies dressed that I liked; it reminded me of how my older cousin Sharon dressed, she used to hang around with Hells Angels. As I began silently admiring their clothes, I also noticed that the woman had a nice-sized spliff in her hand, which I was equally admiring. Just as I was getting lost in my thoughts, I noticed a pungent stench filling the carriage. I was confused for a moment, and then, to my astonishment, I saw a puddle beginning to form on the floor around the woman's legs. She had wet herself! The guy put a comforting arm around her. I felt embarrassed and did not know where to look.

Periodically, I'd heard people talk about how smoking too much weed could turn you mad and I had come across one or two Rastamen who were totally out of their heads. Likewise, I'd heard from people I looked up to that smoking weed could cause you to lose your memory.

The fact that the hippie woman did not have complete control of her bodily functions and wet herself in public, seemingly without a care in the world, left me dumbfounded. I felt that if I gave in to the temptation to smoke and continued giving in to it, I could end up like the hippie woman, or, more to the point, like one of the crazy Rastamen.

At that moment, the whole idea of wanting to smoke weed left me, and after that experience the desire never really returned. I guess my teenage mind – whether right or wrong – linked the hippie woman wetting herself in public to her holding a big spliff in her hand.

The Police Raid That Didn't Happen

Each week, I went to my friends' houses as much as possible to let them know what I had learnt in the Bible. Most of my friends were like me, of Afro-Caribbean descent, and therefore had experienced similar things to me.

I remember being fascinated with the prophecy of Daniel chapter two, partly because I recognised the artwork of the statue of the metallic man, which the church used to help explain the prophecy. The image was identical to one contained in the set of three Bible storybooks my foster mother had put away. I later discovered that the three books were produced by the Seventh-day Adventist Church's UK publishing house the Stanborough Press (SP).

I was keen to understand the prophetic aspects of the Bible because it was a theme mentioned in roots-rock-reggae music. Additionally, topics such as Judgement Day, Babylon and the Antichrist were all mentioned in the music and found in the biblical books of Daniel and Revelation.

I quickly learnt that the Seventh-day Adventist Church pretty much specialised in these prophecies. By studying the Bible, in particular the books of Daniel and Revelation, I got to understand why there are so many different churches and religious organisations; why there is so much suffering in the world and who is responsible for it; and how the world will finally come to an end.

At this point, I had been going to church for around three months. I had just gotten an understanding of the prophecy in Daniel chapter two, where each element of the statue's body represented a future world empire whose rise and fall were predicted with pinpoint accuracy. The prediction started from the Babylonian empire of Daniel's day (605 BC) through to the culmination of the second coming of Christ. This news I had to tell my friends.

One Monday night, I made my usual call around a friend's house where people usually congregated. Unfortunately, they had all gone out, but their girlfriends were all in, so I waited for them.

Within fifteen minutes, they returned from Railton Road, Brixton, better known as Front Line (a street notorious for gambling houses, drug dealers and a host of other suspicious activities). They had gone to buy weed. As they started rolling up their spliffs, I took out my Bible and an A3-sized picture of the image of the metallic man of Daniel chapter two.

I began to explain each part of the prophetic image bit by bit and answer questions as best as I could as we went along. Then one of them, let's call him Gary, left the room. Gary returned shortly, saying that they had been followed by the police and police cars and that police officers were outside. I thought, *I don't believe it! If the house gets raided, I won't be able to get through the key part of the prophecy that explains the divided nations of Europe, followed by the second coming of Christ!* So in my mind I said a quick prayer. "Lord, let me

HEAD OF GOLD
BABYLON
[B.C 605-**539**]

BREAST OF SILVER
PERSIA
[B.C 539-**331**]

THIGHS OF BRASS
GREECE
[B.C 331-**168**]

LEGS OF IRON
ROME
[B.C 168-**AD.476**]

FEET OF IRON AND CLAY
DIVIDED NATIONS
OF WESTERN EUROPE
[A.D 476- **2nd ADVENT**]

Image of the metallic man of Daniel chapter two.

finish." Then I continued sharing what I had learnt of Daniel's prophecy.

Soon, Gary went out again then returned with the news that all the police had jumped into their cars and left. So I got to complete the explanation of Daniel chapter two and the second coming of Christ without my friend's house getting raided!

Later, it dawned on me that the experience had been a close shave. Suppose the place did get raided by the police. They were hardly going to excuse me just because I had a Bible in my hand.

Shaking Table for No Reason

Around July 1981, I went to see a school friend of mine (let's call him Frank) to share my latest spiritual findings. He lived in West Croydon and had an older sister who was into witchcraft. As I was travelling to his house, an inner voice told me not to go. I ignored it and went anyway.

My friend and I were seated at a small dining table when suddenly the table started to tremble.

"Frank, is there an underground line or something that runs under this house?" I asked.

"Don't be so stupid," he said. "You know there's no underground in Croydon."

"So why is the table shaking?"

"The table isn't shaking."

I looked at him, horrified. "Can't you feel it?"

"Strange things happen in this house," he said quietly.

At that point, the penny dropped. It was some form of demonic interference. I silently prayed to God for protection and forgiveness for ignoring His voice. As I prayed, the trembling suddenly stopped. Then the living room door opened and Frank's sister peered in at us. Her eyes were big and round like a ten pence piece. They looked abnormal. She stared at me. I stared at her. She left the room. I said, "Goodbye Frank," as I fled the house.

As I walked towards West Croydon to catch the 68 bus home, I said to myself, *I'm never going back there again. I should have listened to that inner voice.*

Fighting to Close My Eyes

Around August 1981, on a Saturday night, I attended an all-night prayer meeting at Hampstead Church. This would be my first experience of attending such an event, so I was rather intrigued to see how the night would pan out.

There were about 100 people in attendance instead of the usual 450 to 500 people who attended church for the Saturday morning services. The singing was vibrant, harmonious and melodic. After we had sung a few hymns, somebody announced that we would split into small groups and have our first prayer session. The pianist played a soft melody while everyone slowly moved into groups of seven to ten people, a mixture of teenagers, middle-aged, and senior citizens.

I decided to join a group at the front right-hand side of the church. Each person in the circle prayed. As soon as one person ended their prayer by saying amen, the person next to them started their prayer. Everyone had their eyes closed, but I could not close my eyes. As much as I tried, my eyes just would not close!

I can only put it down to evil spiritual forces trying to distract me from participating in the prayer session. Each person prayed, and soon it would be my turn. I tried as hard as I could to close my eyes, but they would not close—my best efforts resulted in my eyelids fluttering.

Eventually, it was my turn to pray. In my heart, I said, *I need help, Lord,* and with one final attempt, I managed to close my eyes. At first, it was a fight to keep them closed, but the more I prayed audibly the easier it became to keep them shut until finally the sensation of wanting to open them just melted away.

This experience taught me that there is real power in prayer, power to make a difference and change things in your life.

A Letter from Senior Management

In July 1981, I had been working at the electronics company Clifford & Snell for a few weeks, and it was coming up to the time when serious Rastas celebrated Selassie's birthday. On his birthday, no dedicated Rastaman would work. Instead, Rastas would listen to music and smoke all day. I thought about asking for the day off but decided against it. *Rastafarianism was no longer for me.*

However, a few weeks later, I learnt that I would need to finish work early on Friday during the winter months when the UK clocks turned back to keep the Sabbath properly. (Note: I finished work at 5.00 p.m. and sunset was as early as 3.52 p.m.) I spoke with Michael's father, Mr Herman Lunan, who was one of the leaders in the church. He coached me on how to approach the situation.

I asked Mr Pearson, the production manager at Clifford & Snell, if it would be possible to get the time off and make it up some other way, like working through my lunch breaks or working late one or two evenings of the week. He refused, saying, "We can't change the policy of the whole company just to suit one individual."

As a last resort, I asked if I could use my holidays and take a half-day each Friday afternoon. Thus, I would have just enough holiday to cover the fifteen Fridays when sunset was earlier than when I'd formally finish work at 5.00 p.m. That said, I'd have no holiday to use for anything else, but that was a secondary matter. Mr Pearson's response was that he thought I was putting my head in the sand and not solving the problem long-term. Finally, however, he consented and signed my holiday forms.

At the end of December 1981, all employees got what I assume to be the annual end of year letter. When I opened mine, I could not believe what I read. The company had decided to reduce the number of hours employees were to work each week by closing the factory early on Fridays without lowering our wages. That meant I no longer had to use my holidays to get the Sabbath off! Was the change in working hours luck, coincidence or providence?

Seventh-day Adventists will acknowledge the beginning of the Sabbath (Friday sunset), usually at home, by holding a worship service. This typically consists of informal worship: singing a hymn or two, Bible readings/study, discussion and prayers. In homes where children are involved, the approach to worship differs accordingly and includes Bible games, quizzes, storytelling and videos.

That Friday night, I went around Michael's house for worship.

I said to Mr Lunan, "I got an end of year letter from work today, and it said that from next year the company will close early on Friday."

His eyes lit up; he repositioned himself on the edge of the sofa and called to his wife.

"Myrtle, Myrtle, come quickly and hear what Derek has to say."

Mrs Lunan stepped out of the kitchen into the dining room. I shared the news with her, and her face beamed with a smile.

Clearly, they had been praying for me as a family and were over the moon to see how God had answered their prayers as well as mine.

PRE AND POST-BAPTISMAL BATTLES

Chapter 8

"You might have to fight a battle more than once to win it."

Margaret Thatcher

Former UK Prime Minister

Getting Over a Few Hurdles

I'd been going to church each Saturday for approximately three months (July to September) but kept it secret from my parents. I would also go around friends' houses to discuss what I had learnt from personal Bible studies, Sabbath school or the midday worship service.

Some of my friends said it was not for them, but I found it encouraging that others admired the stance I took and actually came to church with me on occasions, while others said they respected what I was doing and wished they could do the same. Furthermore, speaking about the Bible and being questioned gave me the thirst to study even more.

One of the key topics I had studied was baptism. I understood that it involved being fully submerged in water. There is nothing magical about the water or the ceremony itself. The act of being submerged under the water is symbolic of dying to the former mindset and lifestyle; being brought up out of the water is symbolic of being resurrected to a new and fresh perspective and a new way of life. I felt ready because I had experienced a demonstrable change in my life as I got more involved in spiritual activities.

A baptism was coming up on the 26th of September and I wanted to be part of it. If done correctly, everyone who gets baptised demonstrates that they are committed and understand the fundamental teachings of the Church. I had gotten a head start on this because the Sabbath school booklet we were studying that quarter was entitled "This We Believe", and I fully embraced it.

My family thought I was mad and did not understand what I was doing and why. Finally, my mother wanted to take me to a psychiatrist. I said I'd be happy to go only if she and the psychiatrist first read and explained to me the latest edition of the *Focus* magazine that happened to feature the prophecy of the metallic man of Daniel chapter 2. *Focus* is a monthly magazine published by the Seventh-day Adventist Church that discusses a range of biblical topics. After that, my mother did not raise the subject of visiting a psychiatrist again.

I met with Mrs Fleming Noel, the Bible worker at Hampstead Church, to discuss getting baptised. I think it was clear to her that I was serious about my religious conviction and that I loved the Lord, so there was no reason to cover that ground. However, as we spoke, she gently asked me about my dietary habits, particularly if I ate pork (by that time I had become a vegetarian). She also asked whether I smoked, drank or had a girlfriend, to all of which I replied, "No." Despite all of this, she advised me to wait a while as I had only been attending church for a few months.

Looking back, I suppose there were concerns I might've been rushing into baptism prematurely and that I might've been going through some sort of fad, the enthusiasm of which would fade away, leaving me to revert to old habits, which would end with me leaving the church. Nevertheless, I had made up my mind that I wanted to be part of the baptism in September.

Even though Mrs Fleming Noel advised that I'd be better off waiting, I believe that, behind the scenes, Mr Lunan must have pushed for me to be baptised because I was informed that I could be baptised in September. That said, because I was seventeen (probably considered a minor), Mr Lunan insisted that I tell my parents about my baptism and invite them to attend.

After I told my mother, she agreed to come along but was none too pleased about it all. Finally, I felt like all hurdles were out of the way.

Being Strangled

I woke up one Sunday morning and as I lay in bed I felt hands around my throat squeezing my windpipe. The hands felt as if they were under my skin and I struggled to breathe despite no one else being in the bedroom with me. I wrestled with removing the hands that were not there, and finally, in desperation, I managed to mutter, "Jesus, help me!"

Immediately, the strangling stopped. I wiped the tears from my eyes and, whilst shaken up, managed to do my usual routine and go out for the day.

While I did not focus too much on this experience, I felt an opposing spiritual force tried to deter me from being baptised.

Years later, I found out that other people had experienced similar happenings, but I pretty much kept my experience to myself.

Todd and Gillian moved to South Norwood from East London around 1976/1977 when I was in the second year of South Norwood High School. Todd and I became good friends as he blended in with the school posse I was part of.

Both Todd and his sister Gillian experienced something similar. They would feel a force on their bodies as they lay in bed, preventing them from moving. They would only be released when they too called on Jesus to help them. For me, it was a one-off; for Todd, it happened over a period of a week; it still happens periodically to Gillian even up to this day.

My Baptism

The baptismal service was held on a Saturday afternoon on the 26th of September 1981. Usually, the church was half full for the afternoon programmes, but it was standing room only on this occasion as friends and relatives of those getting baptised were also in attendance. The deacons (church caretakers) had rolled back the carpet on the lower platform and lifted a hatch to expose the baptismal pool, roughly 1.2 m deep and 4 m long by 3 m wide, which had been freshly filled with warm water.

Thirteen of us were going to get baptised. First, we all changed from our regular clothes into temporary outfits provided for us: the men wore white shirts and trousers while the women wore blue gowns with white trimmings. We all sat in the front row.

When it was my turn to get baptised, I felt slightly nervous being the centre of attention but confident it was the right thing to do. I was the second person to enter the water.

I remember getting up from my seat and walking onto the lower platform and down the steps into the pool. It's traditional that someone will say a few words about the person being baptised and read their favourite or chosen Bible text. Pastor Benifield, an old English gentleman who was Hampstead's full-time minister, performed the service. I recall him whispering to me instructions on how to position my hands on his arm. He then raised his right arm and said words to the effect of:

"Derek, because of your profession of faith in the Lord Jesus Christ I now baptise you in the name of the Father, in the name of the Son and in the name of the Holy Spirit. Amen."

He then lowered me down into the water so that I was totally submerged and then he brought me back up.

Derek being Baptised by Pastor Benifield 26th September 1981

When I came up out of the water, I sensed the deal between God and I had been officially sealed. I was now formally a son of God. It sounds strange to say, but I felt that God was with me and had been guiding me for quite some time, specifically to Hampstead Seventh-day Adventist Church.

Post Baptismal Battles

As previously mentioned, I was fostered at nine months old and grew up in a white British family. My brothers and sisters were into pop, rock and a little soul music, often listening to artists and groups like 10cc, Wings, Genesis, David Bowie and Wizard.

Watching *Top of the Pops* in my house was a weekly ritual. My older brother and sister, along with their friends, would come around to watch it. The three highlights of the show were what the dance group Pan's People were wearing, what song they would be dancing to and which song had made it to number one.

My older brother and sister eventually moved away and my younger brothers and sister pretty much followed in their footsteps by liking the popular music of the day.

As mentioned, on Friday nights, I used to go around to Michael's home for Friday night worship. The time of sunset would determine what time I would return home. Irrespective of when I returned, I would go upstairs to get a good night's sleep, ready to go to church the following morning.

Just before I started going to church, I used to like going to listen to one particular reggae sound system. They were called Stereograph (named after one of the top sound systems in Jamaica). They were a new sound system that had broken away from another Brixton sound, Soprano-B. Stereograph knew how to blend different reggae music genres and entertain a crowd all night long.

One Friday night, when I returned home after worshipping at the Lunans' house, my younger brother Robert (whose bedroom was directly below mine) started to play tapes of Stereograph playing in dance halls on his ghetto blaster. I was unaware that Robert listened to reggae music, especially cassettes of top sound systems playing in dance halls or nightclubs.

As the music played, I began to recognise the DJ's voice speaking on the mic and was familiar with how Stereograph mixed the music.

I knew that if I allowed my mind to be absorbed with reggae music, particularly sound systems playing in dance halls, the desire to smoke weed, along with a host of other things, would be resurrected. Resurrected desires would eventually reverse my spiritual growth. So, I lay in bed that night with the sound of Stereograph along with other top sound systems reverberating through my bedroom while I prayed myself to sleep.

How Do I Stop Swearing?

I grew up in a home where swearing was the norm. As a result, swearing became ingrained in my mind and vocabulary. A few of my school friends used to say that I swore too much.

When I started going to church, I naturally stopped swearing. I can only put the change in language down to the fact that I had started systematically praying and reading the Bible. However, internally I still uttered profanities freely and frequently. This became a problem for me because I knew it was wrong, but I just did not have the power to stop it.

One morning, as I was reading the Bible, I came across a short verse in 1 Thessalonians 5:17, which said.

"Pray without ceasing."

It was as if a thousand lights switched on in my mind. *"That's the answer!"* I said to myself. I needed to spend the day praying on this particular issue and nothing else. I had also previously read a text where Jesus, in Matthew 17:21, said,

"This kind only comes out by prayer and fasting."

So, I decided to spend the day fasting and praying as I did my work. It would be relatively simple to do because I spent all day building electronic equipment while sitting at a workbench.

So, the day began. I swore in my mind, so I immediately counteracted it with a prayer, asking God for forgiveness and the power not to swear. I then swore again, so I repeated the prayer:

"Father in Heaven, please forgive me for swearing and give me the power to think clearly without cursing."

I'd mentally swear again and again, so I prayed again and again. This became painful because every time I swore I'd feel guilty. It was like someone was controlling my mind without my permission. This went on all morning.

At break time, a few work colleagues walked over to my bench, one of them said, "Hey, you coming to get a bite to eat?"

"Na, I'm gonna stay here today." I thought to myself, *I need to stay focused, keep my mind clear and pray for mental strength to break the habit of swearing.*

Throughout the afternoon, the cycle of mentally swearing and praying continued. Eventually, it got so bad a tear or two rolled down my face.

Two middle-aged women who worked on the shop floor with me walked by me during the afternoon tea break.

One asked, "Are you, alright, son?"

I just nodded my head and put on a smile.

The battle of swearing and praying carried on until the buzzer went at 5.00 p.m. It was time to stop work and clock out. Again, I swore then quickly counteracted the cursing with a prayer. I followed through with another prayer and still another. It then dawned on me that my mind was clear, free from foul language for the first time that day. The swearing had not just subsided; it had ceased.

I sat at my bench and thanked God. I then got up and slowly walked to the washroom to clean up. It felt like I was walking on air.

I clocked out and walked out of the factory towards the bus stop to catch the 157 double-decker bus home. I was running late because I had spent time at the end of the shift praying at my bench before taking a slow walk instead of the usual quick pace walk to the washroom. As a result, I now had to run to catch my usual bus. If I missed it, the next bus was normally too full to get on.

I saw the bus pull up at the bus stop in the distance and a queue of people boarding. I dashed for it. As I approached the bus doors, the driver closed them in my face and just looked at me.

I peered at him through the closed doors. It was like the devil was saying to me, *"You see! All this praying and fasting business has caused you to miss your bus. Curse the man. Spit on the door and kick it down!"* Believe me, six months prior, cursing the driver would have been what I would have done, but then a few Bible texts came to mind:

"Bless them that curse you and pray for them which despitefully use you – bless and curse not."

Luke 6:28 coupled with Romans 12:14

I looked up at the bus driver again. He looked at me. I stepped back.

Then he opened the doors and said, "Jump on board. I was just testing you to see what you would do."

I prayed and quoted the scripture, *"Get behind me, Satan,"* and then thanked Jesus.

Christianity works—not because the driver opened the door but because I did not mentally or verbally swear at him. Prayer works.

STANDING UP FOR THE TRUTH

Chapter 9

> **"Life isn't worth living until you have found something worth dying for."**
>
> Martin Luther King
> Civil Rights Leader

You Seem Different

A few weeks after my baptism, I returned to college to continue my studies. I had completed the first year of my course by studying City & Guilds part one in electronic engineering and half of part two full-time.

To complete the course meant returning to college one day a week for the next two years. This was called day release. Not everybody passed part one, and not everybody returned to Carshalton; some opted to go to different colleges. However, I stuck with Carshalton.

Before I returned, I cut my hair and shaved. While I did not have dreadlocks, my hair was quite long and scraggly, by the standards of the day.

It was my first day back at college. I walked into the canteen where people hung out before lessons started. There were a host of new students but a few familiar faces also.

A girl who recognised me from the previous year approached and said, "You seem different."

She invited me to sit at a table with her friends, who were all in the second year of their two-year full-time course. These girls had not taken any notice of me in the previous academic year.

One of the girls said, "You've changed—there's something about you that's not the same."

"It's not just the haircut," said another.

"Come on, what's happened?" added a third.

"I'm now a Christian and got baptised in the Seventh-day Adventist church," I said.

To my surprise, some of them got excited and began asking all sorts of questions; others did not believe me.

I left the group of girls and made my way to the first lesson of the day. As we waited outside the lab, one of my classmates, Martin, from the previous year said, "You've changed."

Then someone turned to Martin and said, "He seems less mouthy for sure."

Before I could respond, the lecturer turned up and the class began.

Raymond Edwards sat next to me and asked, "What's going on? You seem different."

"I have been baptised and become a Seventh-day Adventist," I said.

He refused to believe me and kept saying throughout the class that I was lying. Scornfully, he told me his aunt was an Adventist and described the type of activities she did (fasting, praying and going to church, etc.). He refused to believe that I would do the same kinds of things.

The following week, when I returned to college for day release classes, I brought a photograph of my baptism as proof to show to Raymond and the girls who did not believe me. During the first lesson, Raymond sat next to me again.

I pulled out the photograph along with the baptismal certificate and said, "Here you go."

Raymond looked at the photograph, his mouth and eyes were wide open.

"I don't believe it!" he said. "It can't be true. What happened? You! A Seventh-day Adventist? Nah, that's not possible."

161

He invited me to his house to meet his parents and sisters. He had told them about my change of character and wanted me to validate my story.

Honesty Is the Best Policy

Despite the Sabbath miracle I had witnessed at Clifford & Snell, I soon grew frustrated with the job and wanted to get a better one—one where I could utilise what I had learnt at college. Olrick had gotten a job at Carshalton College and tipped me off to an opening that came up as a technician at the same college in which we had studied full-time for one year and were now attending on a day release basis. At Clifford & Snell, some guys had completed the three-year City & Guilds course and they were doing identical work to me.

Each week on payday, one of my work colleagues used to ask me for money, claiming that he needed it to pay his bills. But of course I never gave him a penny. I felt that if I were to stay and follow the same career path as them, in two to three years, I would be no better off than they were—short of money every payday. So, I applied for the job at Carshalton College and got an interview.

The problem was that I had used up all my holiday to get Friday off to keep the Sabbath; I could not take time off to attend. I was stuck and did not know what to do. There was no way they were going to give me a day off. In the end, I decided to go to the interview (absent without permission—not something I would recommend).

There were two interviews on the same day. The first went well, but I can't say the same for the second. I remember the vice principal of the college asking why they should employ me when Laker Airways had recently gone bankrupt and the college was getting applications from technicians who used to work there. I fumbled my way painfully through that question. That being said, I was offered the job that same day!

The next day at Clifford & Snell, the shop floor manager, Mr Mikey, came down from his office and started to whisper to Ken, my supervisor.

Mr Mikey was probably in his mid- to late-thirties, around six foot, slim build and swaggered around the place in his suit and tie as if he owned the company. On the other hand, Ken was close to retirement, around five foot five, had grey balding hair and wore a white overall over his shirt and tie. They then both approached me.

"I noticed you didn't clock in yesterday; you were absent," Mr Mikey said.

My heart started to pound, my throat dried up, and I began to feel hot. "Yes."

"So, where were you?" he asked.

I was used to lying at school to get out of trouble; it came naturally to me. But reading the Bible had changed me. I wanted to practice being a good and upright person and had learnt to be honest even if it would cost me.

"I went to an interview for a technician's job at Carshalton College," I said.

Mr Mikey's face went beet red! Ken frowned. I gasped.

"I know!" Mr Mikey said. "They've just been on the phone asking me for a reference." He then looked straight into my eyes. "You're lucky you told me the truth; if you had lied, I would have fired you on the spot." He then turned around and strutted off back to his office. Ken strolled back to his desk.

I sat back at my bench and thought, *Good job I told the truth, otherwise Mikey would have probably phoned the college back to say I was sacked for lying.*

That experience taught me the value of following the biblical principle of honesty.

Not Everyone Liked My Diet

Working at Carshalton College was an eye-opener for me. There was a mixture of black, white and Indian technicians. The hierarchy of qualifications for studying electronics part-time while working was City & Guilds (one year full-time followed by three years' part-time study); the next level up was an Ordinary National Certificate (ONC), which took three years to complete part-time. ONCs were done by those who achieved good grades at school. Then, if you passed the ONC you could do a Higher National Certificate (HNC), which took two years part-time. Finally, the top qualification was a BSc degree, which would be a three or four-year full-time commitment.

I thought I had done quite well to pass my first-year City & Guilds exams, but when the black technicians, who were three and four years older than me, found out which qualifications I was studying for, they weren't too happy. As previously mentioned, the City & Guilds qualification was ranked the lowest in the hierarchy of qualifications. They felt I should be more ambitious and aim higher. One of them was in the final year of his ONC, intending to go on to do an HNC and then a degree. The other had completed his HNC and was doing A-level maths to get into a university, and the other was doing an equivalent of a part-time degree. They insisted that I transfer to do an ONC and follow through by doing an HNC at the first opportunity.

There were nine technicians, and traditionally we would all go on tea break together. On one occasion, while everyone was ordering bacon rolls, coffee and tea, I ordered something like an orange juice and a cheese roll.

One of the white technicians turned to me and said, "What! No bacon butty?"

"I don't eat bacon."

"Why?" said another.

"It's unclean meat and you can get diseases and parasites from it."

A few of the technicians rolled their eyes. Another looked at me with a smirk on his face.

"Why don't you drink tea or coffee?" a third technician asked.

"I don't drink caffeinated drinks, it's not good for you—it's a drug, it's addictive, a stimulant; it picks you up and then drops you down."

The smirks turned into sniggers.

"So, do you eat meat?" someone else added.

"No, I'm a vegetarian."

The sniggering turned into laughter and mocking. I quickly drank my juice, ate my roll and left the canteen to go back to the lab to get on with some work.

Soon after, but before the other technicians arrived, Delton (one of the black technicians) entered the lab and advised me that if I wanted to get on in life, I had better learn to fit in with the others and eat and drink as they did. Needless to say, that was not going to happen.

A few weeks later, one of the other black technicians, Seyi Ogun, approached and said, "Hey, what you said the other day in the canteen about caffeine and not eating pork..."

In my mind, I thought, *Oh no, not another lecture on fitting in.*

I said, "Yeah."

"I went to the library and checked out everything you said—it's all true. Where did you get all that information from?" asked Seyi. (This was the early 1980s when we had no access to the internet or encyclopaedias running on computers.)

"From magazines and books at church and the Bible."

That was the beginning of many in-depth discussions we had about health, lifestyle and spirituality.

One day, I told Seyi that Croydon Seventh-day Adventist Church had asked me to give a talk on drugs at their youth campaign (a series of spiritual meetings that have a common theme, usually held over a few weeks). I invited him along, and he said jokingly that he would come, sit at the front of the church and stare at me to put me off as I was speaking. I challenged him to come and try ... and he did!

The evening I was scheduled to give the talk, I drove with Seyi about five miles from college to Croydon Seventh-day Adventist Church. There were about fifty to sixty people in attendance, the majority being late teens to mid-twenties, mostly huddled at the front of the church, which could fit around four hundred people.

The programme consisted of items from the Croydon youth choir, a soloist, the talk I gave, and a sermonette by Bobby Barker. Before Bobby preached, all the visitors (Seyi being the only one that evening) received a gift handed out by Michelle Edwards (Johnson), a Bible study textbook called *Your Bible and You*.

Seyi brought the book to work the next day and informed me that he did not have a Bible so he could not study the lessons in the book. So, the following day I gave him a spare Bible I had. Before the end of the week, Seyi had started studying the Bible along with the textbook.

Every day, Seyi had a few questions about what he had read. Consequently, we spent time each lunch hour discussing and studying the lessons together.

One day, Seyi said, "I'd like to go to church and see what it's like."

"Let's go to Hampstead this week."

"Don't be ridiculous, I'm not travelling across London just to go to church." Seyi lived in Lewisham (Southeast London).

"Didn't you used to go across London to go to Phebes and Cubies and All Nations?" I asked. These were three nightclubs in North London, about ten miles from where we lived in South London.

"That's different," said Seyi.

"Why?" I replied.

"Isn't there a church in Lewisham?"

"Yeah, let's go this week," I said.

"Just tell me where it is, I don't need you to take me," Seyi said.

"Whatever. I'll get the address."

I was not surprised that Seyi decided to start attending church each week. His questions indicated that he was on that trajectory. Moreover, I saw a gradual change, not just in his dietary habits but also in his mannerism and attitude.

Each Monday morning, we would share notes on how the Sabbath services we had attended went, what we had learned and what we had experienced. After a few months of attending church and studying, Seyi decided to get baptised.

Lewisham Church (in the 1980s) had a seating capacity of about one hundred and fifty people. Needless to say, on the afternoon of the baptism, the church was packed, standing room only.

I had invited Raymond Edwards to Seyi's baptism. He came mainly because Lewisham Church was the church his aunt attended. We managed to get seats near the front of the church.

Seyi wore the same style of clothes as I did when I was baptised two years previously—a white shirt and trousers. The singing was loud and vibrant, akin to the singing of

English football fans at a stadium when their team outplays the opposition. There was altogether a celebratory atmosphere in the church. Not too dissimilar from the feelings of supporters at a political rally have after hearing that their candidate has won an election. I felt incredibly humbled because I had contributed to Seyi deciding to be baptised and join the church by just being myself at work.

Pastor Charles conducted the baptism. Several people were getting baptised on that day. Seyi was the last person to enter the pool. After Seyi was baptized, he went off to get changed. Pastor Charles remained in the pool and began to address the congregation. I distinctly remember him saying that a tear had rolled down Seyi's cheek just prior to him being immersed in the water. When he said that, I felt empathy and emotion for my work colleague, who had become my friend and was now my spiritual brother. Pastor Charles then continued to address the congregation with a few words encouraging everyone to consider finding out more about Jesus.

Raymond, who was sitting next to me, twisted and turned in his seat. When I spoke to him afterwards, he said he did not want to go down the route of Christianity. I respected his decision and did not pursue the matter.

I marvel that a negative experience of being mocked and put down for being a vegetarian and not drinking coffee resulted in someone not just following suit but actually becoming a committed follower of Jesus and being baptised in the Seventh-day Adventist Church.

As time progressed, Seyi told his mother and older brother about the truths he had learnt and they, in time, joined the church and got baptised too.

Over the years, I have periodically looked back and considered how things would have turned out for Seyi, his mother and brother if I had decided to compromise to fit in with the other technicians. I can't help believing that God had placed me in Carshalton College, not just to help me get a suitable qualification and improved career prospects but to reach Seyi, who would go on to reach many others.

A few years later, we both left Carshalton College and went our separate ways but used to meet up every so often at church events. Seyi got married and had children.

One Saturday afternoon, around twenty years after leaving Carshalton College, I was at Wimbledon Church and a mutual friend told me that Seyi had died of a heart attack at London Bridge train station.

Seyi and I had not spoken for years. We had always promised each other that we would both take the day off work and just spend the time catching up, but now it was too late! I felt a combination of shock and sorrow. I went for a short walk to process it all.

The next day, I phoned another mutual friend, Roger, who attended Croydon Church and used to work with Seyi. Roger and I frequently shared stories and we both agreed that he was a great guy. I remember picking up the phone and wondering how I was going to break the news to Roger.

I gently probed to see if he had seen or heard from Seyi; I then said, "I've got some bad news for you. Seyi has passed away—died of a heart attack a few weeks ago at London Bridge."

Roger just repeatedly said, "I can't believe it, I can't believe it."

I'm just glad the Lord was able to use me to influence him before he died.

Technicians at Carshalton College from left to right Olrick, Derek, Colin and Seyi 1983/84

Telling the Truth in a Court of Law

One Sunday, around Easter 1983, I was driving home after spending the morning up in Hampstead, knocking on doors and collecting money for a charity called ADRA (Adventist Development and Relief Agency). I drove a 1969 white Mini 1000cc. I was two miles from where I lived when a car pulled out and hit my car. Both vehicles were damaged but could still be driven. My guess was that the driver of the other vehicle (let's call him Mr Dell) was pulling into the block of flats adjacent to the road I was driving down.

Later that evening, I went with my father down the side road to the flats where I suspected Mr Dell had attempted to turn in. I found his car and took a detailed description of the damage done.

Weeks later, a policeman unexpectedly knocked on my door and asked to interview me. My parents were in the living room with me, but the police officer asked them to leave us alone. Then, after asking a few questions, the policeman stood up and asked me to stand up too and said words to the effect of, "I'm charging you for driving without due care and attention. You do not have to say anything, but it may harm your defence if you do not mention when questioned something you later rely on in court. Anything you do say may be given as evidence."

I felt horrified. *How can this be happening to me? I'm innocent, yet I'm the one being summoned!* In former years I had often experienced being harassed on the streets by the police. I knew exactly what to do in such circumstances, but the sheer audacity of him walking into my home and summoning me to court when I was innocent made me feel sick and mentally paralysed me. I could not think straight.

I called out, "Dad!"

My Dad re-entered the room, shortly followed by my mum, who had a cigarette in her mouth.

"I've just been summoned—what should I do?" I said to my dad.

"Tell him you didn't bleep, bleep, bleep do it," my mother said.

"I didn't do it. He hit me; I'm innocent," I said.

"Is that all?" my dad asked the policeman.

"Yes, sir."

My dad held his arm outstretched towards the door.

I was not removed from my home or asked to attend a police station because it was deemed a minor traffic incident. I was just told I'd have to go to court.

Eventually, I got a date to go to court, which clashed with my holiday to Jamaica. So I wrote apologising for not being able to attend, explaining that I'd be out of the country on holiday and the date that I would be back in the UK, concluding that I'd be happy to attend on my return.

My parents drove me to the airport. On the way, I asked my dad to pull over at a letterbox so I could post the letter to the courts.

My mum asked, "Why did you leave it till the last minute to post the letter?"

"I'll be in Jamaica by the time they get it—too late for them to do anything about it," I said.

My dad and I giggled like two disobedient schoolboys while my mum just looked over and smirked.

When I returned from my holiday, I received a letter with a new court date.

My work colleagues advised me to get a solicitor, but after reading the biblical account in the book of Acts of how God gave the Apostles the words to say when brought before the law courts, I felt I could defend myself. God would be with me and would give me the words to say when I needed them (not necessarily a strategy I'd follow today or recommend to another person).

Leading up to the court case, my mother began to prepare me for the possibility that I might lose my driving licence for some time. She understood how the system worked. The chances of a young black boy (nineteen years of age) being accused and taken to court by a young white man and winning were slim. She also advised that I get a bus to court because if I were found guilty and were banned from driving, the police would follow me to see if I would drive home and then I'd get arrested for driving whilst under a ban.

The case was in Camberwell Magistrates Court five miles from my home. I was dressed in my best grey suit, shirt and tie. Mr Dell was dressed in a T-shirt and rough jeans. His lady friend (let's call her Ms Dell) also wore a T-shirt and a mini skirt. Everyone else in the courtroom was dressed formally.

I sat in the courtroom and listened to the few preliminaries and then Mr Dell took the stand. A court official brought a Bible. Mr Dell placed his hand on it, raised his right hand and read the familiar statement.

"I swear that the evidence that I shall give shall be the truth, the whole truth, and nothing but the truth, so help me God."

Mr Dell then began to answer his lawyers' questions. I frantically jotted down notes on everything he said. Ms Dell went through the same process. Then, to my surprise, a young policeman was called to the stand to give his testimony. The policeman had not attended the accident, so where did he come from and why was he there?

Mr Dell's and Ms Dell's testimonies were identical and the, so called, policeman's report substantiated their testimony, which of course did not match my recollection of events. However, all three made the same mistake. They lied about the extent of the damage done to Mr Dell's car. Mr Dell and Ms Dell claimed that I had turned into his vehicle. Their mistake was that if that were true, then it would have been impossible for me to have damaged Mr Dell's car in the multiple places they claimed. I was being framed.

It was now my turn to be cross-examined by Mr Dell's lawyer.

As I approached the stand, she turned to the judge and said smugly, "This won't take long, Your Honour."

"I want to remind you that this is my courtroom," said the judge.

I took the stand and they brought a Bible for me to swear on. The text in 2 Timothy 3:16 came to mind, which says:

"All scripture is given by inspiration of God, and is profitable for doctrine, for reproof, for correction, for instruction in righteousness."

I thought that the Bible should not be used as a tool to try to impress people, to tell the truth. That, coupled with the fact that three people had just sworn on the Bible yet spoken a pack of lies, made me think the Bible was being devalued in the courtroom. So I said it was against my religious beliefs to swear on the Bible. The judge lowered his head and peered at me over the top of his glasses.

They brought a statement for me to read instead. The lawyer then asked me what my occupation was.

I answered, "Assistant technician at Carshalton College of Further Education."

The judge again gave me the same look. Mr Dell's lawyer pushed at me hard with repeated statements that began, "I put it to you that you were etc., etc., etc." The lawyer was trying to insist that Mr Dell was in the process of taking a right turn, was indicating, and that I overtook him and somehow turned into his car.

I kept my answers short and to the point, just like Jesus advised in Matthew 5:37:

"But let your 'Yes' be 'Yes,' and your 'No,' 'No.'"

I guess all the times I had been in trouble at school and had been drilled by the headteachers helped me stay calm under pressure. Conversely, I could tell that Mr Dell's lawyer was getting frustrated because she could not break me down.

Finally, she turned to the judge with an outstretched arm and said in a pompous voice, "Would you mind telling the court then what Mr Dell was doing parked up on the road as you claim?"

I responded by looking at the judge and saying, "No disrespect to you, Your Honour," then I turned to the lawyer and looked her straight in the eyes and said, "and no disrespect to you, madam, but I don't know why Mr Dell was parked there, neither does Your Honour know why Mr Dell was parked there. The only person who knows what Mr Dell was doing there is Mr Dell. So why don't you ask him the question?"

At that, the lawyer slammed closed her folder, mumbled a few words to the judge and sat down.

Then came my turn to cross-examine Mr Dell, Ms Dell and the policeman who claimed to have attended the scene of the accident. I first questioned Mr Dell.

The one single question I had was, "If what you claim is true – that I was overtaking you as you were turning into the side road – then please explain how it is possible that your car received damage along the right-hand side wing and all across the front of your car right up to the left-hand side headlight."

Mr Dell had no answer or explanation. I asked the same question to Ms Dell. She, too, did not respond. I just got a blank look.

I then went to ask the same question of the policeman, but the judge stopped me and said, "Alright. We got the picture."

I summarised by explaining that the only way for the damage to occur, as they explained, was for my car to hit the right-hand side wing of Mr Dell's car, go into a spin and then change direction and spin back into the front of his car.

The judge concluded by saying to me that the charges of driving without due care and attention were serious charges but there was insufficient evidence. So he dismissed the case!

When I got home, I told my parents the news and relayed what had happened. They were both surprised and delighted.

ALL THE WAY FROM NEW YORK

Chapter 10

> **"Two people that have the same wants are two people that should be friends."**

Shannon L. Alder
Author

Our Transatlantic Business Plan

In 1980/81, during my first year at Carshalton College and before I became a Christian, Todd and Gillian emigrated to the United States, New York.

Todd and I were daring, mischievous at school, and willing to take risks to make a little money or get something for nothing.

Todd did not like American cigarettes, so I'd sent him a few packs of his favourite brand. We came up with a plan to set up a transatlantic business. I'd send Todd British cigarettes in exchange for Todd sending me weed, which was much cheaper in New York. My father found the letters sketching out the plan and put an immediate stop to it all.

Fortunately, I Stepped in Dog's Mess

Todd returned, alone, to England in 1982 when he was nineteen; he stayed with his older sister, who still lived in their family home in South Norwood. I've heard him tell the story many times that he was out one night, driving around with a group of guys we were all at school with, when he suddenly thought, *Where's Derek? I haven't seen or heard from him.*

He asked the guys where I was. There was a cold silence; then someone said, "Derek's now a Christian."

At Todd's request, they made a detour and drove to my parents' house. It was midnight on Friday and I was fast asleep, but that didn't stop them from piling into my bedroom. Todd had a hundred and one different questions. I got the sense that he was not just curious but interested.

Todd said that while he was in New York, he became friends with a Rastaman named Meshach, who had introduced him to healthy eating. Little did Todd know that this would be one of the stepping stones God would use to capture his interest in the Seventh-day Adventist message.

The church had arranged for an American preacher, Pastor Dick Barron, to visit England in September 1982 and hold a series of tent meetings on Highbury Fields North London. Back in the '80s, several Seventh-day Adventist churches would often come together, pitch a tent the size of a circus and hold church meetings each night for several weeks at a time. Todd loved attending the meetings, so I did whatever I could to take him there.

One day during the week, Todd phoned me and said he'd like to go to Pastor Dick Barron's crusade.

Croydon Church, which was close to where Todd lived, had hired a coach to take people to and from the tent meetings each night. The problem was that it cost 50p to catch the coach and neither of us had any money.

An inner voice said, *Just go.*

So, I told Todd to jump on the coach and say to Mr Burton (one of the church leaders) to pick me up at my local bus stop, which was on route to Highbury Fields.

I quickly jumped in the shower and got ready to go, wondering all the time how I was going to get money to pay the coach fare. As I opened my wardrobe, I felt deeply compelled to wear my white, short-sleeved Marks and Spencer's shirt, the same shirt I only ever wore to church on Saturdays. My mum or sister would iron my clothes for me and it was freshly ironed and hung up, ready to wear.

As I put the shirt on, I felt something sharp rub against my chest. To my surprise, it was a crisp, new five-pound note in the shirt's top pocket. I was astonished as I knew for a fact that my mum would go through all my pockets before washing my clothes checking for tissues. Neither my sister nor mother would have left a five-pound note in my shirt when they ironed it. The money turned up just in time. I was able to pay for both of our coach fares and have cash left over.

Todd and I hung out regularly; we'd go to Brixton Recreation Centre and play squash with Randel. We'd drive around and spend evenings together—it was like when we were at school, only this time the conversation was not about weed, clubs or how to make money but spiritual things. Todd studied his Bible a lot, and I think I learnt as much from him as he did from me.

He also came to church with me every week. A dear friend, Joyce Audain, who became Joyce Morrison in 1989, was very hospitable and cooked delicious vegetarian meals for my friends whenever I invited them to church. The first time Todd tasted one of Joyce's lunches he could not believe there was no meat in it. I remember laughing when he said, "It tasted so good it must have been made with some illegal ingredients."

Recently I bumped into an old school friend, Kevin Elliot, who some thirty-five years ago (1985/86) would periodically attend church with me. He asked how Joyce was keeping and then began to rave about her vegetarian dishes saying that you would not believe they didn't contain meat.

On occasions Joyce would prepare lunch around her sister Yvette's house. This was 1982 before she became an Adventist. Yvette also had a hospitable nature and opened up her home, treating us as if we were lifelong friends, even inviting us to a family function. Yvette suffered from an illness that took the doctors over five years to diagnose. Meanwhile Joyce gave her two books, *Back to Eden* by Jethro Kloss and *Ministry of Healing* by Ellen G White. She used them as reference books to treat herself and informed her doctors what she was up to. Eventually they diagnosed her with cushions syndrome. One doctor felt that had she not followed the natural remedies in the two books she would have developed other complications, such as diabetes. Coincidentally Todd treated *Back to Eden* and *Ministry of Healing* like college text books and embraced the natural plant-based lifestyle they promoted. However, he says the turning point was when he went to a weekend retreat at Broomhill.

Broomhill was a conference retreat centre that the church owned and we visited from time to time. Over the weekend, we would hold various Bible studies, give presentations and have preaching services.

I was one of the organisers for that particular weekend in question. The programme was planned, but Todd had not fully committed to coming.

The Thursday before the Broomhill weekend, I was in a planning meeting at Hampstead Church and felt strongly impressed to go and secure Todd's commitment to come to Broomhill that weekend.

That night, I drove my white Mini at full speed from Hampstead thirteen miles to South Norwood, where Todd lived.

I knocked on his front door, but he was not in. So I turned my car around and went to look for him.

When I reached the end of the road, I noticed a group of guys standing on the street corner, so I pulled over and asked them if they had seen Todd. They all said, "No," so I jumped back into my car and spun it around. As I was driving back towards Todd's house, a stench hit me. I had trodden in dog's mess.

I stopped the car, jumped out, took out the car mat, and was in the process of cleaning my shoes on the pavement when I saw Todd driving down the road in his Rover 3.5 SD1. I waved him down and we began to talk. I eventually managed to secure his commitment to attend Broomhill.

Group picture at Broomhill around 1984. Todd is circled

In His Own Time

Todd eventually left England, left the church, and moved back to America. However, he says that one day the thought came to him that his soul was worthless without Jesus. That thought was the catalyst that spurred him to start attending church again.

He started visiting Emmaus Seventh-day Adventist Church in Brooklyn, New York, close to where he lived. He attended baptismal classes but told Pastor Calvin Harris that he would get baptised when he returned to England.

That Sabbath, he returned home, picked up an old church bulletin and saw the phrase, "Arise and be baptised." He said that reading changed his mind; nothing miraculous or spectacular, just a simple phrase.

He phoned Pastor Harris and told him of his change of heart. So, he got baptised in Emmaus Church in the summer of 1986. While Todd visited the UK a few times after his baptism, he did not return to live.

Todd married his girlfriend Andrea Hing and brought her into the Church. They have raised three lovely daughters. Todd has served as a leader of his church for many years, and he and Andrea own and run their own health food business.

I wonder what would have happened if I hadn't trodden in the dog's mess.

MY TRIP TO JAMAICA

Chapter 11

"All's well that ends well."

William Shakespeare
Playwriter

A Place to Go to Church

Since I was twelve, my foster parents and I had been estranged from Monica (my biological mother). I was now nineteen. I told my foster mother I wanted to go to Jamaica.

Before becoming a Christian, my dream was to go to Jamaica, where sound systems and reggae music originated; I wanted to enjoy the nightlife. However, after becoming a Christian, I had a 180-degree change in mindset but still wanted to visit the Caribbean island to experience the culture first-hand.

I spoke to my foster mother about it and she said I had an aunt called Ms Green who lived in a place called Jubilee Town, St Catherine, and that I should write to her and ask if I could visit. I was surprised that my mother knew the address straight off the top of her head. So, I wrote a letter requesting to visit.

A few weeks passed and I didn't receive the reply I expected and the idea of visiting fell off my radar. However, about six months later, I got a response inviting me over. We corresponded via letter and agreed on a date for me to visit. Surprisingly Ms Green sent me a return ticket to Jamaica.

My foster mother insisted that I wear a suit and a tie on the flight. She gave me strict instructions that I was not to take off my tie until I had met my aunt. In other words, she wanted my Jamaican relatives to see what a fine specimen of a young man she had raised.

She also anticipated that Monica, who purchased my return ticket behind the scenes, would be there. I had not seen my biological mother since 1976. It was now 1983 and I had been going to church for two years.

The two concerns I had with going to Jamaica for a five-week holiday was where I would go to church and how I would get there. My foster mother knew a bit about where my aunt lived and told me that Jubilee Town was deep in the countryside, a tiny village up in the hills far away from everything.

The only connection I had was a letter that explained she would be wearing the same bright red outfit she was wearing in an accompanying photograph. So I was to look out for her when I got through customs and immigration.

I got off the airconditioned aeroplane and stepped out into what felt like a furnace—at last I was in Jamaica. I had to force myself to keep my suit jacket and tie on.

When I did eventually get through customs, Ms Green and Monica were there. I was greeted with excitement. There was a couple there, Mr and Mrs Mack. They were friends of Monica and she had arranged for us to stay at their house in Kingston for most of the holiday.

While I could not call Monica my mum when speaking to her, I managed to refer to her as my mum when talking to others, e.g. "Did you see where my mother went?" However, whenever I referenced Monica as my mother, it felt like I was saying the grass is orange or the sky is purple. Mentally I kept on trying to correct what I had said—it felt counterintuitive. To avoid calling Monica mum, I mustered up the same strategy I used when I was eleven.

It was evening by the time we arrived at their home. Whilst I was getting settled, I overheard Mrs Mack telling Monica that she and her husband were going to a tent meeting and would be back later.

A tent meeting! I thought. That could only mean one thing, a place to go and worship on the Sabbath.

It turned out that Mr and Mrs Mack, along with their youngest daughter Colleen, had been attending these tent meetings and had recently been baptised into the Seventh-day

Adventist Church. I felt relieved that I had people to go to church with for the five Saturdays that I was in Jamaica.

My First Saturday in Jamaica

Mr and Ms Mack lived with their children in Norman Gardens, Kingston. It was a middle-class neighbourhood and everyone was friendly. Word spread that an Englishman was staying at number twenty-five. Some of the neighbours would drop by to say hello.

I woke up early, had a cold shower outdoors and got ready to go to church. The sun was not yet fully risen, but it promised to be another blazing hot day. We were going to attend the tent meeting that was ten minutes' walk away. As we walked through the front yard to enter the road, I could see dozens of people dressed for church walking up and down Norman Gardens. We walked to the end of the road and saw even more people walking in different directions.

I turned to Coleen and asked, "Where's everyone going?"

"To church."

"Yeh, but the tent meeting is over there," I said as I pointed to the right.

"There're churches everywhere."

I was amazed; it seemed like half the neighbourhood were walking to church while the other half sat in their front porches and called out to those walking past, saying, "Say a prayer for me!"

Visit to Jubilee Town

During the second week in Jamaica, Monica and I went to stay with Ms Green in Jubilee Town. My foster mother had said that Jubilee Town was in a rural part of Jamaica, but I did not quite appreciate how remote it was until I arrived there. The word "town" coupled with Jubilee is somewhat misleading. The area consisted of a small community of between seven and twelve houses in the middle of nowhere.

Monica and I left Kingston early one morning and headed to Jubilee Town. The taxi drove for two to three hours then turned off the main carriageway onto a side road to begin the ascent up the hill. As we journeyed, the road transitioned into a dirt track. The taxi driver asked Monica, "How much further?"

"Just a mile or two," Monica replied.

Thirty minutes later, the dirt track changed into a man-made footpath. The driver said, "I thought you said a mile or two."

"Five more minutes and we will be there," Monica replied.

Fifteen minutes later, we had reached the top of the hill where Aunt Green's house was.

When we got out of the taxi, the driver said, "I'm not coming back; by rights, not even a donkey is supposed to come up here."

Aunt Green was pleased to see me again. I got introduced to a few first cousins: Margarette, who was roughly my age, Olga and Julia, who were about seven to eight years younger than me – they all lived in Jubilee Town – and Marlon, a young boy who was visiting from New York.

Olga and Julia were young girls who were scarcely around, so I did not communicate with them much. Margarette was busy with her toddler but did find time to get me plenty of sugar cane from her cane field. The electricity to the village had been out for some time before I arrived; consequently, there was nothing to do after dark: no television, no radio and no lights to see each other or travel between the sparsely scattered houses.

I was wandering around the area one day when I heard someone call me. It was a young guy looking out of the window of his log cabin, which was situated on the edge of the woodland. He said, "Who are you?"

"Derek."

"Where are you from?"

"England."

"What are you doing here?"

"Visiting my aunt ... Ms Green."

"You look like Cardel—do you know him?"

"He's my cousin," I said.

"He's my good friend... You're lucky you look like him else I'd take your money."

I ignored the comment and just walked off.

Being stranded in the middle of nowhere, bored with nothing to do all day, was bad enough, but adding threats on top of it was the final straw; I now wanted to leave Jubilee as soon as possible.

The following day, I was milling around the house when I heard an unfamiliar voice coming from outside. It caught my attention because the voice sounded like someone whose accent was more English than Jamaican. I heard the man say to my aunt that he was on his way to Kingston. *Kingston,* I thought, *I must go with him.* So I rushed out of the house and politely interjected. "Excuse me, sir, did I hear you say that you were going to Kingston?"

"Yes, that's right."

"How are you getting there?"

"My car is parked a few miles down the hill."

"Do you have enough room to take me?"

We were supposed to spend a few days in Jubilee, but there was no plan that I heard of for how we were going to get back to Kingston; this man turning up seemed like a golden opportunity, a chance that shouldn't be missed.

The man replied, "Well, yes."

I asked Monica and Aunt Green if I could go back to Kingston with the man. They hesitated and then agreed. So Monica and I packed our bags and headed back to Kingston.

We made a day trip back to Jubilee in the final week before my stay.

Looking into a Mirror

It was the first time I had been out of Europe and within the first few days of being in Jamaica I had what I called a delightful cultural experience. All the people working in the airport, the banks, shops, the police, the marketplace, and the beaches were black. The experience was surreal. However, what was more surreal than seeing the multitude of black people in a range of different societal positions was the experience of looking into relatives' faces and seeing a mirror image of myself.

My first cousins from left to right Olga, Margaret and Julia

From left to right Monica, her brother (my uncle) Colin and his wife.
Front row Derek, Colin's daughter Jennifer and Cardel my first cousin.

The Desire Had Totally Gone

One day, while I was in Jamaica, the guys who lived across the road from where I was staying invited me to a dance. They said that Gregory Issacs, one of the top reggae artists of the day, would be singing there. In addition, the ever-popular sound system Stereograph, which the UK sound systems had cloned in name and style, was going to be playing.

Back in the day, I loved Gregory Isaacs' music. But, unfortunately, I had missed out on Gregory's UK tour where Moa Anbessa and Sir Coxsone played because I just did not have the money to go, and that was before I had joined Moa Anbessa.

The guys from across the street tried hard to convince me to go, but I was just not interested. If it had been two or three years previous, then it would have been a dream come true, a goal achieved, and an ambition fulfilled! But now the desire for such things had vanished.

That night, I lay in bed and could hear in the distance the sound of Stereograph playing. Then, finally, I turned in my bed, closed my eyes and fell asleep.

What Were the Chances?

I had a fabulous time in Jamaica, and before I left, Monica gave me the addresses of some cousins who lived in East London (twelve miles from where I lived) and said I should contact them. I felt it would be a good thing to do.

When I got back to England, I wondered how I was going to approach them. All I had were names and addresses—no telephone numbers. I did not relish the idea of knocking on some stranger's door and introducing myself.

The same week I got back, a friend from Hampstead Church, Paul Lee, phoned me and said, "It's my turn to take the afternoon programme in a few weeks. Can you help me?"

"Sure, what's it on?" I asked.

"The Sabbath," Paul replied. "When can we meet up?"

"Come down by me tomorrow if you want. Seven o'clock suit you?" I responded.

"Works for me. See you then."

The following evening, Paul came around as planned. We discussed and studied aspects of the programme he was personally going to present. At the end of our discussion, we prayed.

Afterwards, I said, "When I was in Jamaica, I was given some names of a few cousins who live down your way... I don't know them, never met them...." I then told Paul the name of one of the roads.

"Oh, I know that road," Paul replied.

I looked back at the list of names and addresses and muttered, "Cynthia Morrison."

"I know Cynthia Morrison! I went to college with Cynthia in nineteen seventy-seven! She no longer lives there, she's moved... I know where she moved to," Paul said.

"Before I drop you home can we swing by her place?" I said.

"No problem."

I felt excited about meeting my blood relatives and relieved that I could get an introduction.

We drove twelve miles across London to Cynthia's flat and Paul knocked on the door while I stayed in the car.

Paul came back and said, "There's no answer. I'm not a hundred percent sure I've got the right place."

I felt and probably looked disappointed.

"No worries, I know where her mum and sisters live—it's just around the corner," Paul said.

"OK, let's go," I replied.

Ten minutes later, we were outside Cynthia's mother's house. Again, Paul knocked on the door while I waited in the car.

He came back and said, "This is it—come and meet them."

My excitement subsided a bit, and I thought, as I walked from my car to the front door, that perhaps this was all happening a bit too fast.

I was welcomed in by Cynthia's mother and her brother and four (out of the five) sisters. They did not know that I existed.

One sister said, "He looks just like Daddy."

Another gently held my hand up and said, "He's got hands just like Daddy."

Paul spoke with them regarding where Cynthia lived and realised that he had the right block of flats but the wrong level.

I went back to their house that weekend and they introduced me to Cynthia, who then introduced me to her father and another sister.

Upon reflection, I ask myself is this why I ended up at Hampstead Seventh-day Adventist Church, where I got baptised and faithfully attended each week, travelling past several churches in South London, even one in Croydon, which was a fifteen-minute bus ride from where I lived? If I did not go to Hampstead, the chances are I would not have become friends with Paul Lee and, as a result, would not have met my blood relatives. The arrangement of these events, was it luck, coincidence or providence?

Off to New York

Later in 1985, Cynthia and I spent three weeks with my biological mother in Westbury, Long Island, New York.

I was faced with the age-old dilemma of how to address Monica. However, it was easier than on other occasions because only the three of us were around most of the time.

When in Jamaica, I went to church each Sabbath with Coleen. I invited Monica along, but she did not accept. In New York, I had no one to go to church with and the public transport system in Long Island was almost non-existent. So I insisted that Monica drive me to church. She half-heartedly agreed. The first Saturday, Monica attended the church service with Cynthia and me. The following Saturday, she dropped us off at church and came to pick us up after service.

One day, the phone rang and Monica called out for me to answer it. The person asked for Mrs Campbell. At home, it was customary when answering the phone to shout out the person's name at the top of your voice and say, "It's the phone for you." So I called out and said, "Mrs Campbell, it's for you!"

I realised what I'd done as soon as the words left my lips. I wished I could have rewound the scenario and done a take-two, but it was too late. When Monica came off the phone, she looked me straight in the face and said, "I'm your mother ... never call me Mrs Campbell!"

I did not answer. But I thought to myself, *This can't go on.* Looking back, I can see it was a genuine Freudian slip, but at the time, I did not fully understand what was going on in my mind.

Monica would huff every time I did something she disapproved of and mutter under her breath, "Mrs Prudence."

After the telephone incident, I had a long conversation with my biological mother; I apologised and let her know that I held no grudges, malice, or bitterness.

I said, "If it were not for Mrs Prudence, I would not have gone to Jamaica, we would not have met up again, and I would have grown up resenting you. Mrs Prudence periodically explained that you love me, that you are my mother and that what you did was out of love but it was done in a peculiar way."

Monica gently nodded, took hold of my hand caressed it using both of hers. She did not say a word.

Monica and I had reconciled. We never really became close, but there was no resentment between us.

LATER YEARS

Chapter 12

> **"Looking back at my life's voyage, I can only say that it has been a golden trip."**
>
> Ginger Rogers
> Actress

A Comment at a Train Station

One morning in 2010, I was on the way to work; I boarded a train at Wallington, my destination London Bridge.

As I sat in my seat, in my mind I began thanking God for everything He had done for me, I was going through the key milestones in my life in chronological order and eventually reached my experience of falling down the steps in 1981. My sprained ankle had possibly prevented me from getting into serious trouble.

Then I recalled the text in Romans 8:28:

"And we know that all things work together for good to those who love God, to those who are called according to His purpose."

Just as I finished reciting the verse in my mind, the train driver's voice came over the distorted intercom.

"This train is terminating at Norwood Junction, apologies for any inconveniences caused to your journey."

There were low-pitched groans and sudden moves to fetch bags from the overhead racks, which delayed a group of fidgeting passengers from moving down the aisles to exit the train. Some commuters headed straight off while others spent a few seconds waiting for the notice board to update. Meanwhile, I took out my Blackberry phone and started to write an email to work to say that I might be late.

The board updated, and suddenly the remaining commuters moved on. I soon found myself alone on Platform One. The next few trains would get me into London Bridge with time to spare so I abandoned sending the email and slowly made my way to platform four to get a connecting train.

I soon came face-to-face with the steps that I had slipped down as a result of the kids doing star jumps in front of me.

I stopped. I had not seen or used those steps since the '80s. I thought back to the incident in question and pondered how that painful experience of a sprained ankle had kept me safe.

Just then, two railway workers walked past me.

One turned around and said, "Mind you, don't fall down those steps."

Why would a stranger say something like that to me? I thought.

The Steps at Norwood Junction Train Station (September 2021)

As I contemplate the past forty plus years, the negative experiences that transformed into positive outcomes, the times when my innermost silent thoughts corresponded with physical happenings and meeting the right people at the right time, I ask myself if it were a stream of good luck, a series of chance coincidences or a sequence of divine providences that guided me through my teenage and later years. I think the latter.

"Once you've made a decision, let providence be your" guide.

Morgan Freeman
Actor

ABOUT THE AUTHOR

Derek Morrison was born in 1964 in London, England. He is of Afro-Caribbean descent and was fostered into a loving, white, atheist family when he was nine months old. In *Luck, Coincidence or Providence?* he retraces his personal journey through racism in the 1970s and '80s; his embracement of roots-rock-reggae; and his eventual acceptance of the Seventh-day Adventist Christian faith.

Derek and his wife Joyce have two adult children: Gregory and Gabriella. *Luck, Coincidence or Providence?* is Derek's first book.

www.derekmorrison777.com

www.instagram.com/derekmorrison777

derekmorrison777@yahoo.com

Thanks for reading! Please add a short review on Amazon and let me know your thoughts

Printed in Great Britain
by Amazon